COMMUNISM:
A WORLD WITHOUT MONEY

Un monde sans argent: Le communisme was first published by
Les amis de 4 millions de jeunes travailleurs, 1975–6.

The drawings on the cover of this book, and on the first
page of each tract, were modeled off of the illustrations
in an anonymous Spanish edition of Tract 1. Originally
digitized by the defunct Editorial Klinamen, it is now
archived at <u>mortarpress.com</u>.

Translation © A. Jinha Song, CC BY-NC-SA 4.0.
Mortar Press, 2026, Philadelphia, PA.

ISBN: 978-1-957112-27-5

COMMUNISM:
A WORLD WITHOUT MONEY

by

FRIENDS OF 4 MILLION
YOUNG WORKERS

Translated from the French
by A. Jinha Song

Mortar
Press

CONTENTS

TRANSLATOR'S NOTE

A. *Jinha Song*

Un monde sans argent: Le communisme was published serially, from 1975 to 1976, by ultra-left communist Parisian collective Les amis de 4 millions de jeunes travailleurs. It was soon thereafter translated into English by the Socialist Party of Great Britain, which in 1979 produced a very short excerpt of Tract 1 for its monthly *Socialist Standard*. A full English translation would not appear for another thirty years, when anonymous <u>Libcom.org</u> users Alias Recluse and Craftwork took it in turns to upload an apparently original translation, chapter by chapter, from 2011 to 2016. Pattern Books would publish that version in 2020 as part of its Radical Reprints series.

This Mortar Press translation is my attempt to fully render the strangeness and humor that I most enjoy about *Un monde sans argent*. As it was originally published as a series of tracts, it bears all the energetic language, inconsistency, idiosyncrasy, and occasional rhetorical expediency one might expect from the format. I've resisted smoothing all of that out wherever possible. In practical terms, this has ranged from honoring some very peculiar syntax, to directly representing the consistently gendered and sometimes ableist language, to maintaining the authors' own format for citation, irregular as it is. They were indifferent bibliographers at best; all footnotes are original to this translation, meant to supplement the text's sparse citations and, less frequently, provide cultural context for the contemporary Anglophone reader.

On context—one of this text's great shortcomings is its analysis of what it describes as the "primitive," a typically imperial muddle that reaches across millennia to confound early humanity with New World indigeneity. Using footnotes to hold the text to account for this matter would have exceeded the scope of my project, but I felt compelled to provide more context here:

1. The notion of the indigenous Americas as a sparsely populated wilderness is largely a European invention, a backwards generalization of post-contact numbers that does much to obscure the genocide of 95% of the continents' population. In fact, recent estimates of pre-Columbian population density range 7 to 12 times higher than the scholarly consensus at the time this book was written. For an history of these estimates as imperialist ideology, see Shepard Krech III, *The Ecological Indian: Myth and History* (New York: W.W. Norton, 1999).

2. Another useful European invention this text employs is that of the indigenous person as the passive beneficiary of natural resources. This invention was among the earliest ideological justifications for colonization and dispossession. For a recent perspective on active indigenous land management, see M. Kat Anderson, *Tending the Wild: Native American Knowledge and the Management of California's Natural Resources* (Berkeley, CA: University of California Press, 2013).

Thanks to Patrick Germain, invaluable collaborator and meticulous reader. And, always, to Ian.

TRACT I

1.

WHAT IS COMMUNISM?

Communism is the negation of capitalism—a movement produced by the very growth and success of the capitalist mode of production—a movement that'll eventually topple capitalism and bring forth a new kind of society. Where there exists a world built on the wage labor force and the commodity, there has to come a world where human activity is never again subject to wage labor, and where the products of that activity are no longer objects of commerce. Our time is the time of this metamorphosis. It brings together the elements of the capitalist crisis with all the materials necessary for a communist resolution of this crisis.

To describe the principles of communism; to consider how they make it possible to safeguard the future existence of humanity; and to show that they're already at work, right under our noses—these are our objectives.

Science fiction?

We'd like to depict that which will be tomorrow's world, the communist society we envision. This is absolutely not about challenging science fiction, or journalism, by writing a report on the lives of the men and beasts of the future. We have no time machine to climb that hill.

Despite the appeal of the question, we can't predict who's going to prevail in the war that pits the slacks against the skirts, vegetable broth against bird's nest soup. If worst comes to worst, we can't even say whether humanity has a future. Can anyone promise that we won't be blown away in a nuclear war or a cosmic cataclysm?

That said, prediction remains desirable and possible. We intend to describe communist society on the basis of its general laws of operation while paying particular attention to what distinguishes it from present-day society. We have to show that it's possible for tomorrow to be something other than an improved or repackaged today.

To avoid being too tedious, we'll occasionally go into detail; we'll provide examples. These shouldn't be taken too seriously. You're free to think up different ones. You're free to reject ours.

Tomorrow isn't neutral ground. Capital aims to occupy and subjugate all social space—but unlike the imaginings of science fiction writers, it can't shuttle the commerce of its commodities and its wage workers between past and future. It takes its revenge in the realm of advertising and ideology. We're invited to live today on tomorrow's time, to buy here and now the clock or the car of the future. Successive, competing, and sometimes "anti-capitalist" notions of a capitalist future muddle our present.

To discuss the communist organization of society, despite the risks of error, is to begin lifting the lead weight that hangs over our lives.

The old question of the reactionaries—*But what do you propose as an alternative?*—needs to be rejected out of hand. We aren't idea peddlers. We don't have to market-launch a replacement society the way you would a new pocket watch. Communism is an object neither of commerce nor of politics. It's the radical critique of both. It is not a plan put forward, even democratically, for the choice of voters or consumers. It's the hope, for the proletarianized masses, to no longer be reduced to the status of voters or consumers. Anyone who assumes the position of spectator, who'd like to be able to judge without having to commit to anything, is barred from the discussion.

If it's possible to speak of revolutionary society, it's because revolutionary society is already gestating within present-day society.

Some will find our theories entirely insane or entirely naïve. We don't hope to convince everyone. It'd be disturbing if that were possible! In any case, there are those who'd rather gouge out their own eyes than recognize the truth of our positions.

The proletarian revolution will be the victory of naivety over a servile and dessicated science. Those who demand proofs should beware. They run the risk of being shown these proofs, not in the calm of the laboratory, but violently, and on their backs.

Before saying what communism is, we first have to clear the ground. We have to denounce the lies surrounding it—to say what it isn't. For while communism is an extremely simple reality, so linked to everyday life that it can feel almost palpable, the most enormous untruths haven't failed to proliferate around it. This is only a paradox for people who are unaware that, within the "society of the spectacle," it's precisely the sense of the everyday and the familiar that must be repressed.

2.

COMMUNISM OR CAPITALISM?

According to popular opinion, communism is a doctrine first elaborated in the 19th century by celebrated Siamese twins Karl Marx and F. Engels, to be perfected a little later by Lenin, founder of the Soviet state. It'd be applied to more or less fanfare in a certain number of countries: the USSR, Eastern Europe, China, Cuba... It's in this context that people debate whether the regimes of Yugoslavia or Algeria are socialist, capitalist, or mixed. You can rest assured—or be sorry—that we won't be singing the praises of this socialism here or that communism there. We don't think the moon's made of green cheese; we don't mistake the desolate gray of Eastern Europe, or the delirium of the personality cult in China, for humanity's radiant future.

Sliced bread

Communism was founded neither by Marx, nor by Engels, nor by Ramses the Great. There might be a brilliant inventor behind sliced bread or gunpowder; there isn't one behind communism, any more than there was behind capitalism. Social movements aren't a matter of invention.

Engels, then Marx, met with a movement already well aware of its own existence. They never claimed to have invented either the thing or the word. They didn't write much on communist society itself. They helped communism, in movement and theory, to emerge from the mists of religion, rationalism, utopianism. They spurred proletarians to stop relying on the plans of one or another reformer or the revelations of one or another visionary.

True revolutionaries don't fetishize the ideas of Marx and Engels. They know that the ideas were the products of a particular era and that they have their limitations. Both men evolved; both sometimes contradicted themselves. It could be argued that everything's to be found in the work of Marx. Still, it has to be possible to sort out!

We don't claim to be Marxists. But to those who do claim to be Marxists, we deny the right to appropriate and falsify the thoughts of their heroes.

The proof that great men are powerless to the movement of history is given us in the sordid way that the works of Marx and Engels have been distorted in order to be used against communism.

There are individuals more gifted and more far-sighted than the bulk of their peers. Class society cultivates these differences. They have repercussions within the communist movement. We aren't engaging in discussion in order to determine whether it's the leaders or the people who make history. We're saying that the work of Marx—like that of Fourier, or Bordiga, or whatever other spokesperson for communism—surpasses the point of view of the mere individual. Communism doesn't deny differences in ability, nor reduce its theorists to mere loudspeakers for the masses; to the contrary, it is the fierce and constant enemy of careerism and celebrity.

Communism is neither an ideology nor a doctrine. Just as there are communist acts, there are also communist words, texts, theory—but the action isn't the application of the idea. The theory isn't a pre-established plan for a struggle, or a society, most suitable for massaging into reality. Communism is not an ideal.

The countries that proclaim themselves Marxist-Leninist aren't areas where the principles of communism have been poorly applied, for one reason or another. They are capitalist countries. Their regimes present some idiosyncratic characteristics, but they're just as capitalist as any liberal regime. You could even say that countries like Poland or East Germany are much more capitalist than many less-industrialized countries of the "free world." In these "communist" countries, they combat certain natural tendencies of capital; this is done for the sake of the general development of capitalism and is in no way a defining feature.

There's nothing communist about the command economy, or collective ownership of the means of production, or proletarian ideology. These are aspects of capitalism that were intensified in those countries. All the fundamental characteristics of the system and all the logic of capital accumulation, re-baptized as "socialist accumulation," do very well there.

The capitalist mode of production

To see socialism or communism in Marxist-Leninist regimes is to misunderstand their reality; above all, it demonstrates an ignorance of what capitalism is.

People think that it's based on the power of a very specific class, the bourgeoisie; on the private ownership of the means of production; on the frantic pursuit of profit. Not one of these features is fundamental.

The bourgeoisie is heir to the archaic mercantile class. After ages of playing a powerful but strictly delimited role within agriculturally-based societies, over the course of the European Middle Ages the mercantile bourgeoisie began to control not only mere commodities but also the instruments of production. Among these was human labor power, which it transformed into a commodity via wage labor. This is the origin of capitalism.

The bourgeoisie came to power the moment it became the dominant class, thanks to the power of the economic and industrial forces that sustain it—forces that rendered the old methods of production obsolete. But it can't do anything but submit to the laws of its own economy. The owner of capital, it must obey this force that drags it along, shoves it around, and sometimes drives it to bankruptcy.

The individual and the business have some room to maneuver, but neither can swim against the current for long.

No class, in times past, has ever been able to satisfy all of its whims by using the ostensible forces at its disposal. Even the most undisputed tyrant can only persist by circumventing the narrow limits of his actual sovereignty. It's a mistake to seek to explain social phenomena in terms of power. This goes even more for capitalism than it does for the systems that preceded it.

The class of capital's administrators has seen itself endlessly reshaped by the very effects of capital. What does the wealthy merchant of the Middle Ages have in common with the modern manager? Their motivations and their tastes are different. This is necessary to their ability to fulfill the same function at two different moments in the development of capital. The class of feudal lords situated itself through tradition and heredity. This no longer applies for a bourgeoisie that unmakes and remakes itself by way of achievement, marriage, and bankruptcy.

The relations that bind the slave and the master, the serf and the lord, are personal relations. The modern proletarian, on the contrary, is bound less to a boss than to a system. What shackles him isn't a personal allegiance or some specific coercion; it's precisely the need to survive, the tyranny of his own needs. The proletarian, uprooted from his feudal lands and alienated from the means of production, has no recourse but to go and prostitute himself. He's free, marvelously free. If it should strike his fancy, he could even refuse to go sell himself and so starve to death.

A bourgeois or a politician can go bankrupt on a personal level. In Russia and China, it was a whole sect of the international bourgeois class that was left high and dry. It saw itself replaced by a bureaucracy. Don't mistake the latter as some radically different class! A "communist" banker or captain of industry bears more resemblance to his capitalist enemy than either does to his "ancestor"—not of the 15th or 16th century, but of 50 years ago.

If capitalism, be it Western or Eastern, can't be explained by the power of the bourgeoisie, communism can even less be reduced to the power of the proletariat. Its advent signifies the self-destruction of this class.

Private property

The private ownership of the means of production isn't a constitutive characteristic of the capitalist mode of production. It falls within the legal sphere. In the East, it subsists in the peasantry's patches of land. In the West, it's being eroded by public property.

The state is often the owner of large industrial outfits. The postal services and the railroads, in being nationalized, haven't shed their capitalist natures. F. Engels saw, in this state tendency to assume ownership of the productive forces, a general evolution that would relegate private capitalism to antiques shops.[1]

The development of modern capitalism is increasingly tending to disassociate the ownership from the management of the productive forces. Even bosses—not only of nationalized companies but also of sprawling private enterprises—don't own the capital they control; if they do, they own a tiny fraction of it. The capital needs of industrial giants far exceed what could be furnished by a personal or family fortune. These entities operate on the money furnished by a functionally impotent mass of petty shareholders and individual savings accounts.

The condition of Eastern Europe must be understood in accordance with this general evolution of capital.

---

1 "Whilst the capitalist mode of production forces more and more of the transformation of the vast means of production, already socialized, into State property ... it creates the power which, under penalty of its own destruction, is forced to accomplish this revolution." Engels, *Socialism: Utopian and Scientific*, trans. Edward Aveling (Chicago: Charles H. Kerr & Co., 1908), 126-127.

Profit

The capitalist is supposed to be propelled by the quest for maximum profit. The expression "maximum profit" doesn't mean much. A business owner can try driving men and machines at full capacity for one day, or for a week, or even for a whole month, if he's sure of finding a market. But he runs the risk of immediate regret, having exhausted all his capital. A failure of this kind took place in China with the "Great Leap Forward." Neither the rate of economic growth nor the scale of generated profits, and thus the determination of shareholder and administrator income, are freely decided by all-powerful capitalists.

Making money—that's what propels the capitalist, whether it be to hoard or to invest. If he fails to do so, out of laziness, out of generosity, or because it's no longer objectively feasible, his enterprise will be eliminated. This also plays out for the bureaucrat, mingled with the fear of administrative sanctions. Neither in the USSR nor in China do they proclaim that profit has disappeared. On the contrary, they seek profit for the good of the people, for the development of communism. It's become an instrument of economic measure, in the service of the planned economy!

As Marx has shown, capitalist development cannot be explained by the profit motive in either the East or the West. It's the opposite that's true. The ideas of profit and property rent don't explain the workings of the system. They're only the categories through which the ruling classes become aware of economic necessities and are driven to act.

Unlike the left-wing humanists who see, or pretend to see, profit as their great enemy, revolutionaries don't allow themselves such delusions. We don't reproach the system for its immorality. We don't cling to archaic fields that are no longer profitable.

Profit will disappear with the revolution. And without delay! But until then, it has a role to play in protecting workers, to a certain degree. It imposes limits on the tyranny of bosses. It obliges them to steward their human assets. If it were possible to abolish profit while preserving capital, the average business would turn into a concentration camp and society would slide into utmost barbarism. Nazism isn't an accident of history. It's the unleashing of forces that continue to lurk in the slums of capital's civilization. Profit sets some limits on the authoritarianism, the will to dominate and crush, engendered by an inhuman system.

So go after profit! But you also have to go after every part of a society in which human life itself has become a commodity.

Wage labor and industrialization

The capitalist mode of production is built on two solid pillars distinguishing it from the modes of productions that preceded it.

The first of these pillars is wage labor. There have always been men who rent out their charms, their political attachments, their military abilities, and even their labor power. But all this remained marginal in social systems composed of small groups, among whom money and commodities didn't circulate much. The development of capitalism signified wage labor's true introduction to the field of production. It would turn it into the general form of exploitation.

The second pillar is industrialization, or more broadly, a mutation in man's relationship with nature and his own activity. Man is no longer content to scratch at the soil to eke out his subsistence. From here on out, he undertakes to systematically transform nature on a constantly increasing scale. Capitalism is an uninterrupted revolution in the methods of production. It's the progress of science and reason in the face of fatalism and obscurantism. It's the movement that succeeds the stagnation of agrarian societies.

Communism won't turn the ship around. The end of wage labor doesn't mean a return to slavery or serfdom. Overcoming the process of the "conquest of nature," and of the industrial organization of labor, doesn't mean returning to the stagnation of the past. Communism will abandon the aggressive and chaotic nature of capital's undertakings. Its goal isn't to destroy, compartmentalize, and subjugate, but to act comprehensively on the world so as to humanize it, so as to render it habitable. Beyond industry, it will reconcile the necessary and the pleasant. It will rediscover, on a higher level, the lost familiarity that once united the human being with his environment.

Capitalism didn't come into bloom one fine morning because people suddenly realized how efficient it was. It isn't some triumph of reason. It imposed itself on the fly, through social convulsions that were often cruel and irrational. It provoked mutinous reactions. It had to retreat before pressing onward. It fished its wage laborers out of the masses of peasants that it had previously driven from their lands and reduced to the status of beggars.

The movement of capital has a dual aspect. On the one hand, it's the development of human and material productive forces, and therefore of use value and of utility. On the other, it's the development of exchange value. The commodity has always presented these two faces. Capital remains commodity, but it's moreover a value that unceasingly seeks to inflate itself.

Capital has long been emerging from beneath the commodity. The merchant could, through his ingenuity or his craftiness, maintain and turn over an ever-growing hoard of goods. The moneylender could do the same, troubling himself only with money. But these primitive forms of capital couldn't go on indefinitely. Value remained parasitic, not able to create the means necessary to its own accumulation. It was only by taking hold of and fixing an ever-growing value on the means of production that capital has really been able to flourish. A vampire that feeds on value, which is to say human labor, it needs to cultivate mechanization and productivity in order to achieve its aims. For capital, these are only means. For us, they're what matter most in the end. These technological developments often take nasty forms—unemployment, deadly weapons, the ravaging of nature—but they'll make it possible to revolutionize human activity, and to emerge from the barbaric era of class society.

Communism doesn't cut down capital so as to rediscover the original commodity. Market exchange is a link in a progression, but it's a link between antagonistic parties. It'll disappear without anyone having to revert to barter, that primitive form of exchange. Humanity will no longer be divided into opposing groups and enterprises. It'll organize itself to convert and make use of its shared heritage, to distribute duties and pleasures. The logic of sharing will replace the logic of exchange:

1. Money will cease to exist. It isn't a neutral instrument of measurement. It's the commodity in which all other commodities are reflected.
2. Gold, silver, and diamonds will no longer have any value beyond what's borne by their specific utility. As per Lenin's wish, it'll become possible to reserve gold for the construction of public urinals.

The state and capitalism

In the "communist" camp, money continues to circulate in tranquility. Division by borders, and within these borders the division of the economy into separate enterprises, is doing extremely well.

The State's role in the economy, which is based legally on the public ownership of enterprises, is explained by the nature of capitalism.

The State and the commodity are old friends. Merchants want society to be unified, thieves to be hunted down, and currency to be guaranteed. The State and the bureaucracy find, in the circulation of goods and people, the means to free themselves from the agrarian world.

The modern State, monarchical or republican, is the product of capital's dissolution of feudal structures. In its capacity as the representative of the public interest, it sets itself against the individual's interest. It is necessary to capital because it helps to overcome the contradictions and oppositions that the latter can't help but provoke.

The monarchy and the bourgeois, despite difficult moments, supported each other in the face of the feudality. Political consolidation was necessary to the development of commercial and industrial enterprises. Wealth and resources allowed for the power of the State to become stronger and more autonomous. Often, the State even directly intervened to allocate or consolidate the capital necessary for one branch of industry or another. It developed the legal arsenal necessary to the development of a free workforce. It liquidated the customs and constraints of old. By the time the bourgeoisie made its first open appearance on the political scene, it had long since been a dominant force, and the monarchical State had long since come under its service.

In Russia and Japan, countries that were thrown onto the international stage in a state of under-industrialization, it was the State itself that initiated and organized the development of capitalism. It did so to preserve the grounds of its own power, to furnish itself with modern arms. In conscripting capital, it was only bowing to the latter's superiority. The monarchy was embarking on a process that would ultimately end in its own destruction. The conditions necessary to this transplantation weren't present everywhere. If it succeeded in Japan, it's because the state was already autonomous and trade mature. China initially ran aground, and so did the majority of the other precapitalist countries.

The State often has to intervene in order to correct capital, which enjoys demonstrating its own caprice and prefers to settle more in one place than another. Bureaucratic regimes only elevate this tendency to previously unknown heights.

Does Eastern capitalism allow for growth that's more harmonious or rational than Western capitalism? The question doesn't make much sense. If this has happened, it's thanks to the failings of traditional capitalism. If this traditional capitalism is now being reimported to Moscow or Leningrad, it's because of the failings of Eastern capitalism.

Where the bourgeoisie developed slowly by means of the economy, the bureaucracy won political power by relying on the support of specific social forces, like the proletariat and the peasantry. It's still no less the product of international capital's disintegration of traditional society. The bureaucracy had no choice. It wasn't able to establish socialism or communism like it claimed it could. It wasn't able to restore traditional capitalism and make it fertile. This was because of its social foundations and their need of capital. By trial and error, the bureaucracy found a path which was in keeping with its nature and allowed it to accumulate industrial capital at the expense of the peasantry.

The bureaucracy is a unifying force that enabled the authoritarian transfer of wealth from one sector of society to another. It alters the natural development of capital for the sake of its own goals of power and permanence. But capital isn't some neutral force that can be applied in any direction. The bureaucracy plans; it dominates. *But what does it plan, what does it dominate?* The accumulation of capital. It diminishes the free market; it combats an ever-resurgent black market. This is proof, not of its anticapitalism, but of the fact that capital's natural basis is alive and well. What would we say of the gardener who, because he has to pull out weeds, claims that the plants he cultivates are no longer vegetables!

The western States themselves have been led to intervene more and more directly in the interplay of economic forces. They need to have social policy and they need busy themselves with planning. Bureaucratization isn't a phenomenon specific to the countries of Eastern Europe. Democratic and fascist States are just as affected by it as they are by big private firms. It's the product of and dismal remedy for society's increasing atomization.

In one sense, it's inaccurate to speak of bureaucratic capitalism or State capitalism in Eastern Europe. All modern capitalisms are bureaucratic and state-run.

Though the owner of all industry, the State doesn't hold absolute control. Real power and legal power aren't the same thing.

With liberal capitalism, the State can attack one major corporation or another by relying on the support of popular, military, or even bourgeois forces. It is the power. This doesn't allow it, however, to rise above economic laws. It wants to stand against the power of monopolies, but it can't return to the small businesses of the past.

With Eastern capitalism, the bureaucratic state cannot abolish commercial categories or competition between businesses, regardless of its thirst for control. As long as there are separate businesses, they'll compete, even if prices are controlled.

This lack of unity isn't limited to the economic sphere. The bureaucracy itself is ceaselessly divided by factional struggles and interpersonal conflicts. In the absence of unity, the image of unity must be maintained. The enemy is the anti-party, not the party rival next door.

What the bureaucracy gains in efficiency for the economy, it loses again. The lie—the loss of reality—glut the social body. Covert struggles replace open competition.

Though capable of initiating a burst of economic development under thankless conditions, the bureaucracy is in thrall to the technological lead of liberal societies.

Recycling

What interest would capitalists have in calling themselves communists? Capitalists don't like being called capitalists, as a general rule!

This naming convention has a specific origin tied to the Russian Revolution. To call yourself a communist was to claim a devotion to the working class rather than admitting to exploiting it. It can grant a humane sensibility—the construction of communism— to the inhuman development of the system. Elsewhere, they dangle projects of a "new frontier" or a "new society" before the masses!

When capital proclaims itself communist, when it recycles Marx's thoughts in order to disseminate them to the intellectuals in its universities, or to stupefy the workers in its factories, it only apes a movement that, elsewhere, is actually being realized. Capital doesn't create; it recycles. It feeds on the passion and initiative of proletarians, which is to say that it feeds on communism.

You can't understand much about communism if you don't understand the capitalist nature of the countries of Eastern Europe. Revolutionary struggle can't spare Stalinism, which is a fundamentally anti-communist system and ideology. The fact that it has strongholds in the very heart of the working class must not soften us; on the contrary, it should spur us against compromise.

It's a great boon for Stalinism that nobody criticizes it as a capitalist system. Some revolutionaries, especially anarchists, have recognized it as communist—provided that they could append "authoritarian" to the term. Behold the monster, authority! By way of explanation, we'll look to the character of Karl Marx.

The Trotskyists, following their leader, that unhappy adversary of Stalin, have elaborated interpretations as complicated as they are moronic. A socialist base and a capitalist structure can coexist, at least in the USSR.[2] As for other countries, they remain under discussion. In any case, they never understood anything about communism. No more than Trotsky, who saw in compulsory labor a communist principle.[3] They aren't revolutionaries;

---

2 "The Soviet Union is a contradictory society halfway between capitalism and socialism." Leon Trotsky, *The Revolution Betrayed*, trans. Max Eastman (New York: Doubleday, Doran & Ltd., 1937), 241.

3 Trotsky, *The Defence of Terrorism: Terrorism and Communism* (London: George Allen & Unwin Co., 1935), 123-145. No attributed translator.

Trotsky himself was. But he was never anything but a bourgeois revolutionary and unhappy bureaucrat. Let's leave this little clique to its intellectualism, its Byzantine quarrels, and its ridiculous cult of organization.

The Maoists, those "mystico-Stalinists," reduce the whole matter to a question of politics and morality. The USSR has become social-imperialist, maybe even properly capitalist. Happily, China and Albania, under the wise proletarian leadership of Mao, Enver Hoxha, and Bibi Fricotin,[4] haven't been contaminated. Communism: profit and politics, made to serve the people!

As communist ideas spread to fulfill the needs of a proletariat once again becoming revolutionary, even in the USSR and China, these sects will appear more and more eccentric! They try to restrict the role of the revolution to the political stage. They're at the vanguard, but the vanguard of capital. Because during periods of revolution, it's all of these political clowns who'll try to avoid being cast out by putting on revolutionary airs.

It's become a tradition that revolution should be opposed in the name of revolution. Militants who've gone astray among the Stalinists and the leftists will rejoin the true communist party.

Some people, less blind, recognized the division of social classes within Eastern capitalism. Unfortunately, they also thought they recognized in it a new and improved mode of production. This did great honor to Stalin and company.

Savages

We see nothing communist in the regimes that claim to be so. By contrast, we do see it where it's not usually ascribed. Primitive societies—driven back

---

4   Rascally protagonist of the eponymous French children's comic strip, 1924–1988.

by "civilization," subsisting in lands that are barren or hard to access—are communist, though their members live off of hunting and gathering or rudimentary agriculture. Thus, the USSR isn't communist, but the United States of America was, just a few centuries ago!

We don't intend to return humanity to this stage. It'd be very difficult, in any case, because that state of affairs requires a very low population density. It is important, however, to restore primitive and prehistoric humanity.

The Indian was happier and, in a certain sense, more civilized, than the modern American citizen. The caveman didn't die of hunger. It's today that hundreds of millions of humans have empty stomachs. The primitive, as M. Salhins has shown, lives in abundance.[5] He's rich, not because he's accumulated riches, but because he lives as he sees fit. His apparent poverty, his destitution, arouses pity in the Western traveler who sometimes paradoxically marvels at his good health before infecting him with the pox. Primitives possess practically nothing, but for those who live off of the hunt and the harvest, this is no embarrassment. Their destitution allows them to move freely and make the most of nature's riches. Their security is based not in savings but in their knowledge and their ability to make use of what their environment provides. They spend less time earning their living than do the civilized. Their "productive" activity has nothing to do with the ennui that emanates from the office and the factory. Lucky Yir-Yoront of Australia, who have one word for both work and for play![6]

There's a profound difference between the communism of the past and the communism to come. On the one hand, there's a society that makes use of its environment, knowing well how to adapt to it; on the other, there's a society based on the continuous and profound transformation of that same environment. The period of class societies between these two communisms

---

5   Marshall Sahlins, *Stone Age Economics* (Chicago: Aldine-Atherton, Inc., 1972).

6   A factoid much evoked but little attested in cultural anthropology.

will seem, with a little hindsight, a painful but relatively short stage in human history. Thin consolation for those still immersed in it!

Marx and Engels

Marx and Engels strove to understand the development of capitalist society. They were little concerned with depicting the world of the future—an undertaking that had monopolized the efforts of the utopian socialists. But you can't completely dissociate the critique of capitalism from the assertion of communism. A real understanding of the historical roles of money and the state can only arise from the prospect of their disappearance.

If Marx and Engels had little to say about communist society, it's doubtless not just because its distance made it harder to grasp, but because paradoxically, it was more present in the revolutionary imagination. When they spoke of the abolition of wage labor in *The Communist Manifesto*, they were well understood by the people that they were reiterating. Today, it's more difficult to picture a world rid of the state and the commodity because they've become omnipresent. But having become omnipresent, they've also lost their historical necessity. Before they become entirely useless, before what they assert have become truisms, theoretical efforts need to take the reins from spontaneous consciousness.

Marx and Engels may have been outstripped by one Fourier[7] in grasping the nature of communism as a liberation and harmonization of the emotions. Nonetheless, the latter never managed to leave wage labor behind; among other things, he suggests that doctors should no longer be paid in relation to patients and their illnesses, but rather according to the state of

---

7   Utopian socialist Charles Fourier, 1772-1837, who prefigured Marx's theory of alienation in proposing that socialization inhibits inborn "passional attractions."

the entire community's health.[8]

Marx and Engels express themselves clearly enough, however, that they shouldn't be held liable for the bureaucracy and financial policies of "communist" countries. According to Marx, money immediately disappears upon the advent of communism, and producers stop trading their products. Engels speaks of the disappearance of commodity production with the advent of socialism. And don't talk to us about youthful mistakes, as a whole rabble of Marxologists have gotten in the habit of doing. We're referring to the *Critique of the Gotha Program* and *Anti-Dühring*.

All kinds of Stalinists will talk about dross in the work of the masters. They'll make a song and dance of publicizing that they're Marxists, not dogmatists. According to them, money, capital, and the State have all shed their bourgeois natures in order to become proletarian. The most daring go as far as to say that, once communism is established, we might be able to rid ourselves of all those odds and ends. For the others, communism is simply a society in which the standard of living will be very, very high. In any case, communism is lost in the clouds, and the ladder leading there is made up of a profusion of rungs constituting as many transitional stages.

It's correct that they're establishing communism in Eastern Europe. They're establishing it no better nor more thoughtfully than they have anywhere else. A revolution will be necessary to bring that about.

This notion of establishing communism by means of economic and social instruments is characteristically bourgeois. It pictures the thing like the production of a manufactured good. It sees society as a vast factory. It believes that the whole functions like the part. It's all a matter of will, of planning, of the political line...

The mistake these Stalinists make along the way has repercussions on

---

8   Charles Fourier, *Le nouveau monde industriel et societaire* [The new world of industry and association] (Paris, 1829), 541.

the outcome. It isn't a matter of getting rid of the business economy but of turning the economy into one singular business; the waste embodied by the existence of a police force will go away; the strengthening of moral sensibilities, through "communist" education, will be enough to get rid of theft and subversion!

Doubtless, the best solution is the one proposed by Joseph Stalin himself. Failing to transform things, transform the words instead. *Why would you think that people who receive a wage are wage laborers*, pontificates the little father of the people, *seeing how through the State, they own the companies that employ them? You cannot be your own wage laborer! Wage labor is therefore abolished in the Soviet Union. If you are under the impression that you receive a paycheck, if you are afraid of being fired, this is because you are totally delusional. Happily, our socialist fatherland boasts re-education centers and psychiatric hospitals!*

Stalin concedes that commodity production and division into enterprises still exist, but that this cannot be a matter of capitalism, because under capitalism, the means of production are owned by individuals. Everything, in fact, boils down to questions of legal definition. It's enough that a state proclaim itself communist for it to be so.

As Stalin explained this all to us in *The Economic Problems of Socialism in the USSR*, those who have since pored over the issue have contributed nothing new.

You can see Mao Zedong and Fidel Castro as courageous freedom fighters, skillful statesmen. You can reckon that the Chinese have more to eat than do the Indians, and fewer political freedoms than do the Japanese. But all of that still lies within the bounds of capitalism.

3.

THE END OF PROPERTY

Communism is the end of property. It's a well-known affair, and one that arouses a great many anxieties. Some are entirely warranted. Owners of grand estates, numerous luxury residences—they'll be made to moderate their lifestyles. Industrial and commercial fortunes will disappear. Those who are going to be expropriated make up a narrow and well-defined caste, even if they do hold a large portion of society's resources today. Incidentally, as general rule, we won't be attacking individuals; we'll behave according to the nature of the goods in question. We'll seize the castles and leave the cottages alone, whether they belong to the poor or the rich! But the anxieties that have crept into the minds of proletarians, and especially peasants, are unwarranted. Communism is not about taking from the oppressed what little they have left.

What is property?

The question isn't so simple to settle. Witness the polemic that pitted Marx against Proudhon. The latter had posited that "property is theft." Proudhon knew full well that the origin of property wasn't natural. It's the product of a society ruled by power relations, violence, and the appropriation of the labors of the other. Only, if we say that property is theft, whereas theft is defined only in relation to property, we're going around in circles.

The problem grows murkier still when it turns from property to the abolition of property. Should all property be abolished, whether the means of production or personal possessions? Should it proceed on a selective basis? Is it a matter of replacing private property with collective or state property? Is it a matter of radically forgoing all property and what that might look like?

Communism opts for the latter proposal. This isn't about the transfer of property titles but rather the disappearance of property, full stop. In the revolutionary society, people won't be allowed to "use and abuse" a possession just because they own it. This rule will know no exceptions. Buildings, and hairpins, and plots of land will no longer belong to anybody—or if you prefer, they'll belong to everybody. Before long, the very idea of property will be considered an absurdity.

So will everything belong equally to everyone? Will the first person who comes along be allowed to evict me, to strip me, to snatch the bread from my mouth because I'll no longer own either my house, or my clothes, or my food? Certainly not; on the contrary, the material and emotional security of each person will be better protected. Simply put, it will no longer be property rights that are invoked for protection but the direct interests of the people concerned. Each and every person must be able to be sheltered and clothed, to eat their fill of what they like. Each and every person must be able to live peacefully. Some ideologues would prefer to see property as nothing more than the human extension of animal territoriality. Property is thus rendered a phenomenon, not of a given era or even of a particular species, but of an entire branch of zoology. But no one's ever seen a fox or a bear lease out a territory that it owns, or live in a burrow where it's only a humble tenant! But it's a regular thing in our society. It's precisely property that allows for the dissociation of usage and possession.

That a good would no longer be *property* indicates nothing of the use to be made of it. Use will be reverted, precisely, to use. A bicycle will be used for getting around, and not just for Dupont, its legitimate owner, to get around. The question of whether human beings, or certain human beings, need a fixed territory and objects to which they can grow attached, for reasons sentimental or affective—this falls outside the purview of property. And to reassure the dental hygienists: we aren't proposing to communalize toothbrushes.

Pitting individualism against collectivism, personal against social usage, to make it a matter of a "societal choice"—this is complete bourgeois cretinism. From that perspective, it'd be absolutely necessary to take sides with rail transport against the personal vehicle. Communists would be in favor of orgies, and the bourgeois in favor of masturbation! We couldn't care less about those kinds of debate; they can only be settled in light of their practical circumstances. In any case, we aren't the ones hoarding and alienating.

In present circumstances, property rights constitute a safeguard against the destruction of private life. They're a very paltry safeguard. They don't prevent noise from passing through the walls of poorly insulated tenements. They can't do much against an expropriation. The peasant might be the owner of his land; this hasn't kept the countryside from emptying out.

Today, lands lie fallow, houses uninhabited, resources of all kinds fallen by the wayside. All of these could be very vital. Unfortunately, their owners are unwilling or, worse, unable to use or sell them.

The notion of property encompasses a reality; it is also, however, a mystification. You can own something without being able to really control it. The lie is twofold. It's social and economic. It also concerns the relations between men and nature.

Property rights are necessary to capitalism. Trade requires that things be clear-cut. When doing business, it's necessary to know who actually owns the merchandise and who doesn't. Local custom can settle questions of how to arrange matters and use things, but as soon those things acquire a degree of independence from men, passing from hand to hand, custom is no longer enough. Only faint traces of it remain in the countryside: rights of way, of water supply, of gleaning... But commodity and capital need a universally applicable body of rules, independent of the particular nature of any situation.

Land ownership, in the modern sense, didn't exist in the Middle Ages. On any given estate could be exerted the rights of the serfs, of the lord, of his overlord, of the church... Up to the 19th century, some number of rules continued to limit the power of the landowner, who was allowed no more than the first cutting of a meadow, had no right to enclose it, and had to allow gleaning and common grazing.

In the world of bourgeois equality, everyone's a free proprietor—the Eastern European peasant of his fields, the boss of his factory, the worker of his labor power. There is no theft, and yet you can enrich yourself and hoard resources beyond all proportion to what your own labor should make possible. Property conceals the relations of exploitation.

If the peasant-cum-"farm operator" owns the plot of land he cultivates, he nevertheless remains at the mercy of costs whose formation are beyond his control. Working nonstop, he still never manages to get rich.

Property does not explain the power of capitalist business. The business owns fixed capital: buildings, machinery. This doesn't account for the scale of the resources that pass through its hands and constitute its turnover.

The interpenetration of the economy requires the limitation of property rights. As a matter of fact, what you do at your house risks having negative repercussions on your neighbors' houses. You can't get away with dumping your waste in the river just because you own part of the riverbank.

The absolute character of property rights, which according to the Declaration of the Rights of Man are "inviolable and sacred,"[1] doesn't take into account the might and the whims of nature. The most dogged of property owners would be powerless in the face of a volcano cracking open in his house. He could call the police for help, but that wouldn't scare off the

---

1   The Declaration of the Rights of Man and of the Citizen (1789) asserts the French Revolution's Enlightenment ideals. It remains constitutional law.

intruder. Generally speaking, inanimate objects and natural phenomena don't serve at our beck and call.

As remarked by Niño Cochise, grandson of the great Cochise, white men spend their lives fighting over land.[2] Yet it isn't men who can hold the land, but the land, on the contrary, that can hold and nurture men. It ends up burying us all, sooner or later.

The agrarian question

The agrarian question is closely bound to the problem of property and its solution. It's a vital question for the revolution. In the past, armies of peasants have fought against workers' insurrections. The opposite has also happened, as in Mexico, but the little peasant's always been easily mobilized by the counter-revolution in the name of defending his sacred right to property.

In industrialized countries, capital has done the very work that it accuses "the reds" of trying to do: it's driven the majority of peasants from their lands. Therefore, it can no longer count on their frightened masses to constitute the counter-revolutionary army. However, cities continue to rely on the countryside for their supply of subsistence goods. The party of law and order will always be happy to weaponize this situation against the revolution.

Agricultural workers who don't own the soil they cultivate, who are either simple farmers or the employees of big operations, will organize themselves to carry on production. They'll no longer need to answer to their

---

2   This is the only text in which this quote appears, and the identity of actor and memoirist Ciye Niño Cochise (1874-1984) is likewise unclear. His avowed lineage and tribal affiliation are probably fabrications.

former bosses. The land will go to those who tend it! If their former bosses or landlords want to join them so as to contribute knowledge and resources, all the better. They'll only be allowed to do so as equals.

Where the ownership and the cultivation of the soil coincide, where the peasant employs very few wage laborers or none at all, the problem needs to be considered in a different way—for the good of society as a whole, which couldn't easily do without some discontented farmers, and for the good of the peasant, whose condition has proletarianized, who depends on a capitalized system for his supplies and his sales, and who has to understand that he's got everything to gain from the communist revolution.

Capital has developed at the expense of agriculture. It has siphoned agriculture's labor force and resources into industry. Communism will turn this tide. Agriculture is the darling of communism because it directly concerns the production of foodstuffs and the preservation of a livable environment—two things that capital has particularly neglected.

Property, hereditary or not, will disappear alongside the state and the legal system that once safeguarded it. The custom and practice of cultivating a given parcel will remain, and must even be safeguarded by revolutionary authorities. It's on this basis that peasants will be able to band together, or, if they prefer, continue to look after their plots in isolation. It's likely that they'll mingle the two courses of action at least for a while, each remaining attached to their lands but helping each other to perform certain tasks and sell their products. Inheritance, in the strict sense, will disappear—but who's more likely to be qualified and motivated to take over from a farmer than his own son?

The general rule will be to allow peasants to organize agricultural production as they see fit. Coercion would be the worst and most costly solution.

The agrarian collectivization implemented by Eastern European capitalism has nothing to do with communism. Their reasons for collectivizing had less to do with ideology than with class and the economy. It was necessary to combat the spontaneous resurgence of the countryside bourgeoisie.

Rich peasants further enriched themselves on the backs of poor peasants by making usurious loans. This is how a hub of usurious capital accumulation came to be, rivaling the hub of industry on which the bureaucracy relied. It's why it was necessary to impose, and pay the cost of, agrarian collectivization. It was a heavy cost. Peasants in the Soviet Union initially resisted, going so far as to slaughter their livestock. The long-term consequence was a stagnation in agricultural productivity due to the kolkhozniks'[3] lack of interest, hence the fluctuating policy regarding family-owned plots of land. Collectivization shielded the peasants from direct economic pressures and thereby helped to keep them in the countryside. This brought about reduced pressure and competition in the labor market. The USSR preserved a body of peasants that's exceptionally large, in relation to its level of industrialization. It drags them around like a ball and chain.

In renouncing collectivization, are you renouncing the revolutionizing and communizing of the countryside? Absolutely not! Quite the contrary! The communist revolution is the liquidation of the market economy. This affects the countryside, too.

The farmer will no longer make money in exchange for his efforts, if he's a wage laborer, or for his goods, if he's an independent producer. He'll supply society with his surplus production, free of charge. In return, he'll owe nothing for the goods necessary to his subsistence and his work. He'll no longer be driven by the appetite or need for money. His motivation will be rooted directly in his interest in the work, his love of his way of life, or his desire to be useful.

The peasant will see his labors ease. He'll be able to call on an outside workforce for help. This will be made possible by the closure of a whole host of more or less parasitic businesses, and a reduction in the workforces of industry and the service sector. It will be possible, during major agricultural

---

3   Member of a kolkhoz, or a farming collective in the Soviet Union.

efforts, to temporarily halt certain industrial productions in order to free up hands. This is unimaginable today.

It's not only production but distribution that will be transformed. The route leading from farmer to consumer will be shortened as much as possible. Products can be transported directly from any given farm to any given city, and managed by the interested parties themselves. When people see the difference between the costs of production and the costs paid by consumers, they'll appreciate the benefits of such simplification.

Peasants, alone or with help, will perform the labor of cultivating land and livestock. They won't do so autonomous of the rest of society. We aren't promising them absolute freedom. Agriculture currently depends on, and will continue depending on, other sectors of the economy. It has its upstream suppliers of fertilizers and agricultural equipment. Its independence is therefore already restricted in this respect. Besides, it plays too important a role for everyone who depends on it to refrain from ever even sneaking a peek.

To take an extreme scenario: it's naive to imagine that if some farmers were to abandon their land and their livestock, no longer needing to make money, everyone else would happily agree to die of hunger. In this kind of situation, it'd be feasible to pay the freeloaders back by cutting off their supplies. Farmers must be allowed to keep hold of their lands and to live there as they see fit, but they can't be allowed to become parasites or, above all, to stockpile resources that others could use in their place.

It's on the agenda of the revolution to overcome the divide between city and country. This can only be achieved very gradually, because that separation is written in stone and concrete. You can't wave a magic wand and transport skyscrapers here and forests there. It'll be possible, however, to rapidly implement measures in this direction. For example, the temporary or permanent resettlement of urban populations to the countryside, where small industrial centers could be established to complement, and if possible partner with, agricultural efforts. Many people who left the countryside only reluctantly—or who dislike the city—will be happy to go back. Individual and collective gardens will proliferate and brighten up the suburbs, and even the urban centers. To this end, we can tear up the pavements of streets made obsolete by reduced traffic. It'll facilitate the process of recycling certain household wastes; reduce transportation expenses; and supply the population with fresh vegetables. One of the shortcomings of capitalist agriculture is that, having distanced itself from its consumers and their waste, it needs to make up the imbalance through constantly intensifying chemical and biological interventions. In the new gardens, those who are presently refused roles in production and often doomed to boredom—the children, the elderly, the sick—will be able to occupy themselves and feel useful. These will be fertile educational grounds for the de-schooled youth. Finally, something to renew our polluted atmosphere!

From scarcity to abundance

The right to and sentiment for property will die out in communist society because scarcity will have become a thing of the past. It'll no longer be necessary to cling to an object for fear that, should you loosen your grip on it for even a moment, you'll never be able to enjoy it again.

What spells will you cast, to materialize this fantastic epoch of abundance?, the bourgeois will taunt. There is no magic to it. We'll be able to summon abundance because it's already there, right beneath our feet. This isn't a question of generating abundance but of liberating it. Capital, having bent man and nature beneath its yoke for centuries, is what will actually make it possible. It's not that communism will produce abundance but that capitalism maintains scarcity artificially.

The astounding rise in labor productivity hasn't done much, so far, to change the lot of the proletariat. It's even had detrimental effects. The power of capital destroyed the Third World's traditional societies without allowing their populations access to the industrialized world. This, combined with monstrous population growth, plunged the better part of humanity into utter destitution. The position of the wage slave would come to be a veritable promotion, in relation to that of the vagrant.

Nuclear and electronic technologies first exerted their influence as weapons. Happily, scientific progress has delivered us from those barbarous times, back when you were forced to look at those you killed, sometimes even spattering yourself with their blood. Yuck!!!

Even the inhabitants of "rich" countries, who benefit from this increase in productivity, are being cheated. Growing wages and escalating consumption only serve to compensate for deteriorating living conditions. People owning better objects or more of them, as compared to some previous era, doesn't signify that they live better lives. The workman has a car that his father didn't—but his workplace has moved far from the countryside where he spends his weekends. He loses again in traffic jams what was gained in working hours, and gains in nervous fatigue what was reduced in physical effort. What industry grants with one hand, it's already taken back with the other; the conditions of its development make it so. Industry extols the excellence of its remedies but neglects to mention that it's the one incubating the disease. This is no accident. The logic of commodity production presumes that the conditions of dissatisfaction be maintained. Medicine needs disease. As was remarked by C. Fourier: in civilization, scarcity is born of abundance itself, and society moves in a vicious cycle.[4]

Human beings have seen themselves more and more reduced to the passive role of consumers. Their state of undeath is enlivened by the artificial life of commodities. Their misery becomes a rainbow reflection of pleasures, displayed in every shop window and offered at unbeatable prices.

In communist society, goods will be free and freely available. The

---

4   Fourier, *Le nouveau monde industriel et sociétaire*, 43.

foundations of social organization will be rid of money.

How do you prevent resources from being hoarded by some at the expense of others? After a momentary euphoria when people help themselves to existing reserves, won't our society be in danger of sliding into waste and inequality and succumbing, finally, to chaos and terror?

These concerns aren't exclusive to a privileged few with a direct interest in maintaining the system. They also represent the perspective of the oppressed, wound up in the fear that an upheaval could worsen their circumstances. In a storm, aren't the mighty better equipped to survive than the small?

Within a developed communist society, the productive forces will be able to meet all needs. The frantic, neurotic desire to consume and to hoard will disappear. It'll be absurd to want to accumulate; there won't be any more money to pocket or wage workers to take on. Why accumulate dentures or cans of beans that you won't need? If any form of constraint persists at that stage, it won't be in the distribution of products but in their very nature—in the obligation imposed by specific use values. At the manufacturing level, there will inevitably be options to choose and others to reject.

When revolutionary society has first emerged from the edges of the old world, the situation will be different. The revolutionary authorities, the workers' councils, will have to establish and enforce some number of rules to prevent the return of mercantile habits and mechanisms. It might be necessary, then, to limit the cans of beans or pounds of sugar that each person can keep at home. No one can say precisely how long this phase will last. It'll vary according to the greater or lesser poverty of each region. It'll depend on the power and resolve of the revolutionary party. A war provoked by the capitalist party, which would wreak havoc on production and transportation, could only prolong this transitional phase. But if you base your estimate solely on the time required for the communist reconversion of productive forces, it could be very brief. Consider how quickly the American economy was able to transform itself, during the Second World War, into a war economy!

With communism, the character of all production and the nature of the objects produced undergo a radical transformation. The disappearance of exchange value has repercussions on use value.

The transformation of products

The commodities offered up by the market form an extremely hierarchized ensemble. For any given need, there isn't one commodity, or even a handful; there are multitudes from the same brand and its competitors. The aim, of course, is to satisfy the public and respond to the variety of its needs. *The customer must have a choice!* In reality, he has only the choices permitted him by his financial means and social position. Many commodities fulfill the same function but are distinguished by quality and exclusivity. This is the case, for example, with saucepans. Different products can also correspond to different uses—only, these differing uses aren't accessible to the same individuals. It isn't the same people who go about their business by supersonic plane as by bicycle.

This hierarchization and differentiation of commodities reflects the capitalist world's intergroup competition and its extreme inequality in wages and living conditions. They leave their mark on industrial development, where the needs of the wealthy play a guiding role. Some goods, like the automobile, lose much of their utility when they become widely available, ceasing to be the privilege of a minority.

Communism doesn't propose to dress everyone in the same uniform and feed them the same gruel, but it will put an end to this noxious diversification and hierarchization of products.

New goods that are still scarce will at first be used collectively, or on a first-come-first-served basis.

In the realm of clothing, you can suppose on the one hand that a reduced number of quality garments will be produced, though enough to serve all sizes and all typical uses. They'll be produced on a massive scale, and by the most automated means possible. On the other hand, workshops could be opened wherein machines and fabrics would be available for anyone who wanted to craft other kinds of garments for themselves or their friends.

The much-vaunted freedom of the consumer runs into limitations beyond the weight of the doubloons in his pocket. You can pay a fortune and still be swindled on quality. When you don't have a lot of money, you're practically guaranteed to be palmed off with junk. Trickery and the commodity go hand in hand; it's not a long way from salesperson to thief. It matters that the selling points be apparent, and it matters little that they're all appearance. What was once dependent on the malice of merchants, capital practically enshrines as law. It produces the commodity itself. It can therefore act to emphasize its image, rather than its actual quality. We've arrived at a point where engineers calculate and determine the necessary deterioration of objects. It wouldn't do to encumber the market with products that last too long!

Plus, the faster that capital runs, the faster it retakes the form of money—only to lose it all over again by reforming as concrete commodity—the more it rakes in. It reinvests itself, with value added. This tendency leads it to condemn unproductive reserves of resources. Everything needs circulate, fast. Even its investments in buildings or machines need to be amortized as fast as possible; they represent money that's tied up. The capitalist sacrifices technology's possibilities on the altar of finance. He invests in the short term instead of the long term. Quality is cut back and the cost of products raised because investment in the means of production was already cut back. Rapid turnover and superficial variation in product lines are preferable to in-depth technological changes in productive machinery. As testified by the history of capitalism, technological progress does get realized, but it's done by way of economic upheaval and enormous waste.

When the products of human activity no longer take the form of capital, there will be no reason not to build up reserves. They'll assure our security and, acting as a buffer, ease the demands on production and transportation. The need for constant haste, unless necessitated by the actual nature of certain products, will disappear. It'll be possible to make long-term plans and muster the strength for large, protracted investments. Technology will be guided so as to enable the manufacturing of durable objects.

Today, the costs of commodity circulation have grown higher and higher, often outstripping the costs of actual production. "Costs of circulation" doesn't only mean the expense of transport but also that of packaging, marketing, advertising... A significant portion of these costs have little to do with the nature of the products or where they'll be used. It's promotion of the commodity qua commodity. It'll disappear.

Even in the actual costs of transportation, serious savings will be possible. The increasingly marked separation between places of production and places of consumption isn't alien to the capitalist nature of the system. The transport of goods will be simplified. The profusion of enterprises and intermediaries will disappear.

The costs arising from the need to control and monitor things that can be stolen—all matters relating to payment—will no longer have any reason to exist.

In this new world, man won't have to constantly pay for and justify his own nourishment, transport, entertainment. He'll quickly get out of the habit. From this will arise the feeling that he is truly free. He'll feel at home everywhere. No longer under constant surveillance, he won't be tempted to take advantage. Why try to lie or build secret stockpiles when you're sure you'll be able to meet your needs?

Little by little, the sense of property will cease to exist. In retrospect, it'll seem somewhat bizarre and petty. Why cling to an object or a person when the whole universe is yours?

The new man will grow closer to his hunter-gatherer ancestors, who trusted in a natural world that would provide life's necessities freely and often abundantly, who didn't preoccupy themselves with a tomorrow they had no control over anyway. By way of nature, the man of tomorrow will have a world he's molded; abundance will be born of his own hands. He'll be sure of himself because he'll have confidence in his strength and knowledge of his limits. He'll be carefree, because he'll know that tomorrow is his. Death? It exists. But it isn't worthwhile to cry over what's inevitable. What matters is being able to savor the moment.

4.

BEYOND
WORK

Capitalism has unceasingly revolutionized the means of production, but it's been incapable of truly liberating and transforming productive activity. Industrial work signifies the most extreme alienation. The proletarian, in blue collar or white, is chained to his machine or to his desk. He's lost the license to appreciate his work, and the leeway to undertake it as he sees fit, which belonged to the artisan and even the serf or the slave. The impersonal nature of this domination doesn't make it any less unbearable.

Work has set itself apart from all other aspects of life. It dominates them through the fatigue and the stupefaction it engenders and through the salary it secures.

Given the control that modern capital exercises over all social life, the principles of work end up regulating the entirety of existence. The logic of efficiency and production govern "free" time. Everything must be rationalized and made profitable, including pleasure and waste! All are cordially invited to take up the reins of system—within their own established conditions.

Communism is, first of all, the radical transformation of human activity. That's where can we start to discuss the abolition of work.

Work and torture

If there's one word that is neutral, it's certainly not the word *work*.

In French and in Spanish,[1] it derives from the Latin word *trepalium*, which designates an instrument of torture that succeeded the cross. Before coming to its modern generalization, it'd first designate work of a particularly grueling nature, and then work in mines. Today, its meaning has expanded considerably but its boundaries remain unclear. As if to provide itself with a natural justification, *work* ends up accounting also for physical phenomena.

In English, the word originates from a tangible agrarian activity.[2] What now characterizes the term *work* is precisely its abstract quality. It no longer designates this or that specific activity, but rather the activity or effort as such. You no longer plant cabbages, you no longer spin wool, you no longer tend sheep—you work. All work is fungible. What counts is the time spent on it and the wages made off of it. As Marx said: "Time is everything, man is nothing; he is nothing more than the carcass of time."[3]

It isn't the word *work* that we revile but the foul reality it encompasses. Never mind whether the term stays or goes. If it must stay, it'll have to undergo a profound alteration in meaning. Maybe it'll end up designating the pinnacle of pleasure!

In communist society, productive activity will lose its strictly productive character. The obsession with output and efficiency will disappear. Work will merge into the whole of a life transformed.

Such a change signifies the end of hierarchy, of the division between the leaders and the led, of the rift separating decision and execution, of the opposition of manual and intellectual labor. Man will no longer be dominated by his tools or by the products of his own activities. The subjugation

---

1   In Spanish, "trabajo"; in French, "travail."

2   This likely refers to "*werk," a reconstructed ancestor word whose secondary definition has to do with rope and rope-making.

3   From his discussion of man-hours in *The Poverty of Philosophy*, trans. Harry Quelch (Chicago: Charles H. Kerr & Co., 1920), 57.

of nature to the productive process, its monopolization by groups and individuals, will cease to be.

This revolution will be accompanied by a technological transformation. What's at stake is the very nature of industrial development.

Capitalism's parasitic nature is betrayed by the fact that it's possible to sustain social life while shuttering a large portion of businesses. In France, the strikes of May 1968 gave proof to the resources of a developed country. The whole of industry was able to be shuttered for a month with no discernible consequences.

There might be a shortage of bread during the revolutionary period. It wouldn't be attributable, however, to a lack of production capacity. It would be due to specific circumstances. This doesn't at all detract from the possibility of shutting down parasitic industries. Quite the contrary; it makes it more imperative, in order to be able to redirect forces toward vital sectors.

It's not possible to determine beforehand, much less in detail, what will or won't be eliminated. We're convinced the war industry is dirty; it'll have no further reason to exist in a developed communist society. Even so, you can't decide ahead of time that it won't be necessary to develop during some transitional phase!

In any case, decisions won't be made by technocratic committees but directly by the workers concerned. And the threat of lost wages will no longer hang over their decision-making!

If some people cling to useless or even harmful tasks, either out of professional self-interest or for less respectable reasons, they'll be held responsible before the whole of the communist proletariat. The right to property or to self-determination won't be an excuse for cops or financial analysts who'd like to carry on with the routines of their regular little jobs!

Everything that serves finance and the state machine—everything that demands substantial, grueling effort just to meet secondary needs—will be eliminated, or at least profoundly transformed. Products and "services" currently hogged by businesses, like the telephone or electric power, can be redirected toward individual consumption. Buildings and machines can be put to different uses.

It'll be possible to meet numerous needs at much-reduced social costs. Transportation, for example, will be built on a more rational use of both individual and collective vehicles. The demands of the timetable will be greatly relaxed. The need to travel will arise less frequently.

Some activities won't actually disappear, but they will be profoundly transformed. Education will cast off, as far as possible, the doings of specialists. Print shops will leave the service of the major newspapers and begin serving a multitude of small bulletins.

The principle won't be to produce for the sake of producing, or to compete to retain customers, but to reduce arduous and uninteresting industrial labor as much as possible. Shuttering useless sectors will allow society to lighten and diversify those productive duties that remain necessary. Human energy, liberated in this way, can see about new activities.

Children, students, elderly people, and housewives will be able to participate in social activities befitting their abilities, all without becoming a competing workforce on the job market.

These transformations aren't luxuries that the revolution will have to indulge in order to entice the hesitant. They are necessary, here and now, for fighting and gathering forces against the party of capital, which is threatening to stick around for some time.

Science and automation

All these measures provide us with only a vague idea of what's to come. Communism will make use of the material foundations bequeathed by the old world. Above all, it'll further technical and scientific achievements. It'll do so quickly, and better than capital can.

It's considered good form to rhapsodize about the technical progress made since the last world war. Really, it'd be more sensible to be shocked at how slowly scientific discoveries have trickled down to industry. Industry is characterized, first and foremost, by its inertia. It advances when historical "accidents" oblige it to change suppliers or markets; it modifies its technical foundations to evade economic stagnation when interest rates collapse.

Present-day industry subsists by refining inventions and discoveries that date back to dozens on dozens of decades ago. Vehicles based on petroleum energy and the internal combustion engine, for example—like our own state-of-the-art automobiles—are veritable fossils in light of what's possible scientifically. Industry hasn't been able to actually advance either automation or new sources of energy. It could only do so if these were to become profitable from within its narrow point of view.

Communism will be able to get away with building machinery and industrial outfits that wouldn't have been considered profitable by businesses, or even by capitalistic states. It'll see progress as worth the effort, regardless of immediate benefit. Only, it'll often be able to discover this immediate benefit in places that capitalism wouldn't notice it: in the improvements to product quality, the good of research, and the betterment of working conditions.

From capitalism's point of view, it wouldn't be profitable to manufacture a silent jackhammer unless the machine could rival or undercut a noisy jackhammer in price. It would matter very little that the resulting savings would come at the cost of obvious unpleasantness. At the moment of launch, it's not possible to take into account the fact that the silent jackhammer might become cheaper than the noisy one, once its production was fully developed. Why would a business risk going bankrupt or, at minimum, make sacrifices in the name of technical progress or humanitarianism? Communism won't simply take over from capitalism; it will transform science and technology. From servants of an industrial hellscape, knowing or unknowing, they'll become tools of liberation.

Science will no longer be a sector distinct from production.

Capital has a vital need for innovation. It can't bring it forth directly from the productive sector. That sector must stay calm, its imagination chained up. Science therefore developed on its own. It remained marginal for a long time, the work of amateurs. But capital, having more pressing need of its services, had to take it in hand. Under the aegis of corporations and the state, science would become an investment. It would bureaucratize, coming under the yoke of functionaries and administrators. Creative freedom would be kept on a leash.

Depending on who you ask, science is a fairy godmother or a wicked witch. The scientist is a sorcerer turned wage laborer. What is the outcome of critical inquiry seems like the work of magic.

The ideology of production recuperates what it's had to concede to the experimental method. Science appears as a sector producing one special commodity: Information. Knowledge ceases to be the precarious result of specific research, instead becoming a sacred product offered up for the contemplation of the mentally infirm masses.

It's a question of liberating initiative and experimentation in order to restore them to the people. Science must cease to be the possession of a caste of specialists, becoming once more an appetite for risk and for play, the pleasure of discovery.

The "conquest" of space demonstrated the possibilities of automation and electronics. It's only a matter of applying all this technology to the transformation of our daily lives. Automation makes it possible to relieve humans of tedious tasks and charge machines with what should be theirs to do.

The first step toward automatic systems—those that function and self-regulate without intervention, once set in motion—dates back to the time of the Pharaohs, when they were used to regulate the Nile. In modern times, they began to flourish. Automated "factories" began to appear; see the mill near Philadelphia that, from 1784, would receive wheat and transform it into flour without any manual invention. Alongside these machines for automatic production, machines for calculation began to appear. It's in 1881 that the automatic telephone exchange was introduced.

Automation has existed for a very long time. It's nothing but an extreme form of mechanization. Electronics are what will make automation a standard, if not most commonplace, form of mechanization.

Electronics, combined with the control of the major sources of energy, will make it possible to operate remotely and to centralize a great number of operations.

Automation doesn't merely represent the possibility of entrusting machines with tasks that humans are unenthusiastic to perform. It is also, and perhaps above all, the possibility of undertaking what would never otherwise be possible. It enables operations that call for faster reactions and more complex calculations than humanly possible. Machines can act in conditions unsuitable for life. Without automation, the development of nuclear energy and the discovery of space would have been impossible undertakings.

Those who want revolution but don't want to resort to *cursed science and technology* are at an impasse. The extensive destruction of our environment is certainly not independent of technology and its possibilities, but you can't pin the blame on them.

Nuclear energy and information technology may present some very dangerous characteristics; this is a reflection of their power. But that fact only condemns present-day society, which uses them recklessly or enlists them to consolidate its control over people.

Up to now, capitalism has only automated things in a piecemeal way. That doesn't mean it can stop there. Its logic—the necessity of maintaining or recouping a reasonable profit ratio—has to compel it to go further. That doesn't mean that the expansion of automation might be compatible with the continued existence of the current system. Automation's very hypothesis is contrary to the survival of a class society; it renders the proletarian unnecessary. "The automatic machine ... is the precise economic equivalent of slave labor" (N. Wiener).[4] At the furthest stage of mechanization's development, human machines will be rendered unnecessary.

The resolution is therefore either communist revolution or the destruction of the proletariat, which would be reduced to a stratum of welfare recipients—or eliminated outright. The prophets of woe have forewarned us of the second eventuality. But our optimism isn't founded on the humanitarianism of our leaders; history's shown that not even genocide rattles them. We simply believe them incapable of mastering the situation and actually implementing policy. For better or worse, we're governed not by übermenschen with incredible foresight but by cretins, clever at maneuvering but incapable of taking an historic view of events. They are themselves more or less rejected from the productive process. In this affair, the important thing is that the proletariat not show itself to be too weak.

The strength of the proletarians is immense. Their awareness of this strength is extremely limited. The working class has always drawn its might from its place in the productive apparatus. The first stirrings of automation, within the apparatus, have only served to bolster this might. A small fraction of workers and technicians now hold tremendous power in their hands. Economic upheavals risk giving them the appetite to use it.

Neither the bourgeoisie nor the bureaucracy can deny the proletariat without denying itself. It's chained to value, which is to say to the human labor that's the basis of this value. It doesn't want progress for the sake of progress but for the sake of money. If it develops mechanization, it doesn't do so with the ulterior motive of drumming out overly disruptive workers. The proletariat is not a mere instrument of the bourgeoisie. It's also the bourgeoisie's raison d'être. Capital (or work) might reduce man to the rank of machine, but it can't stop being a social relation between classes.

---

4   Norbert Wiener, *The Human Use of Human Beings* (Cambridge, MA: Houghton Mifflin, 1950), 189.

Class society and robotization

All class society seeks to turn human beings into robots, to reduce them to objects whose bodies and intellects can be put to use. When one part of society stops working for its own sake but breaks its back to put food in the mouths of a different fraction of society, this not only means that the former is needing to make extra efforts, but also, and above all, that its activity changes in nature. What interests the master isn't the pleasure or displeasure of the slave, his joy or his anguish; it's his production. Class society is founded on the human capacity to develop goods that can be alienated from their producers for the use of others. The human being is no longer a human being but an instrument. The uniquely human ability for building, and for thinking production through ahead of time, backfires against him and turns him into a tool himself!

The exploiter may be cruel or kind toward the exploited. No sentiments are ruled out. Better still, sentiment is necessary to grease the cogs of the system—but it's only one of the system's limited secondary products. The exploiter might be decent, but he can't stop exploiting. He might be sadistic, but he can't destroy his human assets. When capitalism comes to this barbaric juncture, however, it's been driven to it by economic necessity.

The ruling classes of the past used to graft themselves onto peasant communities. Capital shattered these communities in order to bring a crippled and atomized human material under its rule. A commodity amidst commodities, the proletarian confronts his mechanical competitors on a marketplace of the "factors of production." In this struggle, the machine gradually supplants the man and reduces his role in the process of production.

Communism will upend the nature of this progression. Man will no longer be in competition with machine because he will no longer be a factor of production.

The communist use of mechanization means the possibility of

automating a very great number of activities. This isn't to say that the key to the social question can be found in widespread automation.

The abolition of wage labor isn't the replacement of man with machine; it's the human transformation of human activities by means of machinery. It isn't a matter of reducing the workweek from forty hours to zero, gradually or abruptly, as some pseudo-revolutionaries have proposed. A world where one entirely automated industry, working inexhaustible equipment, could at once supply anything imaginable and desirable—that would reduce man to a vegetative state. It'd be a stagnant universe without adventure, because all that could be adventured would have to be programd in advance.

Regardless of the faith it puts in science, that myth is profoundly capitalist. It considers the separation of working time and leisure time as consummate and natural. It wants to reserve the hell of production for machines and the paradise of consumption for human beings. Depending on how strictly that boundary is drawn, it'd all lead to either a permanent all-inclusive resort or a society of fetuses.

Communism is the end of all separation between working time and free time, between production and consumption, between that which is lived and that which is experienced.

Remuneration

The disappearance of wage labor is enough to shake the bedrock of the old society. The obligation to work in order to survive disappears. Work ceases to be a means of making a living. It no longer plays intermediary between man and his needs. It is the direct satisfaction of need. In this way, it ceases to be work. What motivates action stops seeming like an external obligation, becoming instead an internal necessity: the desire to occupy oneself, the determination to be useful. The dissociation of activity from remuneration—if in *remuneration* you don't include the pleasure that activity can materially provide—needs to go hand in hand with the profound transformation of man. It requires individuals who are responsible for what they undertake. It demands that initiative and intellect be cultivated, that selfishness and pettiness disappear.

It's become customary to attribute all of humanity's ills to the incorrigibility of human nature. It's well-known—*man is a wolf to man*.[5] The phrase explains nothing, but it does demonstrate the contempt in which we humans manage to hold ourselves. It's a reflection of the fatalism that capital cultivates, reducing the human being to the role of spectator in his own development.

The idea of maintaining some kind of remuneration during the transitional period in the form of vouchers distributed in proportion to work hours performed, as Marx proposed, isn't advisable. If the development of productive forces allow for a communist revolution—and they allow for one today—the revolution cannot defer the full implementation of its own principles. A voucher system for remunerating and thereby compelling work would fall short of the spontaneous revolt of the oppressed, of all those who rose up expecting neither power nor money nor reward. It would be favored by bureaucrats, administrators, and all those who would rather supervise and demand action from others. This kind of system could only bridle the proponents of action without managing to bring along their opponents. If you have to force someone to do something, we prefer the method of the kick in the ass. It's more frank and more effective.

We aren't inveterate opponents of the employment of vouchers. It'd be

---

5   Little-used transliteration of Latin proverb "Homo homini lupus est," perhaps popularized by Italian-American anarchists Bartolomeo Vanetti and Nicola Sacco, whose unjust executions were one of the greatest 20th-century causes célèbres. In his last words, Vanetti reflected that "Sacco's name will live in the hearts of the people and in their gratitude when ... your laws, institutions, and your false god are but a dim remembering of a cursed past in which man was wolf to the man."

absurd to leave diamonds up to free distribution! Vouchers can be issued, in such cases, by qualified authorities. When it comes to goods concerning production, the vouchers will be issued by factory councils; when it comes to rare or dangerous pharmaceuticals, they'll be supplied by hospitals or doctors; and so on. These vouchers won't serve as remuneration. They'll play the part currently played by medical prescriptions. Their use will be determined by the nature or the rarity of the goods for which they're "redeemed."

The greatest possible number of goods, especially food, must be made free and freely available, whether under the aegis of revolutionary committees and councils in zones that have come into the hands of the revolutionary party, or by coups de force in unliberated zones. This is the method of distribution that's simplest, least costly, and most pleasant. This is the method best suited for popularizing communism. It'll be better to implement this general rule, even if it means cracking down harshly on abuses, than to get bogged down in distribution by distasteful and finicky audits.

Laziness

Won't that kind of program encourage laziness? If you could abolish the principle of remuneration for work while maintaining the world was it is, this would most certainly be true. Only, communism upends the conditions of life and of work in their entirety.

The revolutionary spirit isn't the spirit of sacrifice, each person setting themselves aside to serve the community. That's Maoism! Communism assumes a certain degree of altruism, but it also assumes a certain degree of egocentrism. Above all, it doesn't pit loving your neighbor against loving yourself, demanding that one be made subservient to the other. We don't love vicars any more than we love profiteers. It's capitalism that makes it so that the individual interest and the collective interest are always in conflict—to give is to give in.

The communist man will be no more prone to resignation than to fatalism. The transformation of mindsets will have nothing to do with pedagogy. There won't be an ideal image to conform to. There won't be a transformation of social structures on one side and a transformation of individuals on the other. It's capitalism that separates things in that way. The proletariat will disalienate itself, and it won't be able to do so without changing the whole world and its living conditions. A few weeks of revolution will throw decades of conditioning into disorder. Cowardice, greed, and stupidity are the results of a specific social state. If the situation that engenders them and lends them a certain utility doesn't disappear, the carrot, the stick, and education can only serve to suppress them. With communism, these flaws will disappear because they'll no longer correspond to anything.

The possibility of there being egocentrists, incurable slackers, or irredeemable incompetents isn't necessarily too serious a problem. The greatest enemy of these people isn't repression but boredom. They can quell a great deal of unwillingness. Men are social creatures; it takes a lot of audacity to bear being useless to your own community. Even now, the parasitic and the egocentric have to fake it, for others' sakes and their own. With the abolition of wage labor, it'll be very difficult to maintain delusions about anyone's activity. Everybody will be judged, not on time spent, but on what's actually been done.

Communism doesn't preclude conflict between individuals or groups. Profiteers risk seeing themselves held accountable. If people support them, and if people fatten them up, it's because they really want to.

Communists have nothing against a healthy sense of laziness. Revolutionary society isn't made for people to work themselves to exhaustion within it. The lazy are only at fault if they demand from others what they refuse for themselves. So let the audacious refuse to be suckered, in their view, but don't let them presume to force their personal preferences on everyone!

Given the replacement of coerced labor with impassioned activity, most of the causes of habitual laziness will disappear. Also to disappear is the irritation that the workhorse feels toward the slacker, which often is no more than envy in disguise.

The lazy people of today won't necessarily be the lazy people of tomorrow. Some of those who currently run around exhausting themselves, spurred by profit, will need our kindness. Others who currently seem incapable of rousing themselves will wake up and run wild.

In developed communist society, mechanization will confer man a great power. Each person will be able to choose his own pace of life. One will exhaust himself in costly adventures and spend more than he gives back to society. Another won't ever do much, and yet society will find itself indebted to him. Nobody will be keeping score.

Once financial incentives have disappeared, won't the spirit of inquiry and invention also vanish? Won't everybody content themselves with doing their little chores in a humdrum little way? It's a mistake to believe that the lure of gain and the spirit of inquiry go hand in hand. The merchant consorts with lies and illusions; the scientist constantly needs to ward them off. Science brings in money and invention pays, but it's often not the same person making a discovery who profits off of them. Even in the capitalist world, money isn't what motivates scientific passion. People pilfer their own creativity and imagination in order to make money.

The allocation of tasks

If it isn't possible to stop laziness, won't our society risk sinking into disorder? Even if there's widespread goodwill, will it be enough to resolve the matter of coordinating all activities? Won't everybody rush to take the nice jobs, neglecting the others before machines have had time to take the reins? In short, everyone doing as they please would lead to disaster!

The idea that modern society is very complex, and that this complexity is inevitable, is very widespread. It isn't a mere illusion. The individual feels himself lost in the capitalist jungle. He can't manage to get his bearings, much less understand how the whole thing manages to function. But it would be a mistake to believe that this impression holds true for all modern societies. The impression isn't necessarily engendered by the multitude of operations and situations which constitute the social whole. It arises from the estrangement between decision-making and coordination on the one hand and action on the other.

This impression of complexity and permanent confusion that capitalist society engenders has had its repercussions on the depictions of a socialist world. People have come to believe that the foremost problem to be solved, in the society of the future, is that of planning and coordination. They've imagined a "plan factory" responsible for surveying the state of the economy and determining technical coefficients that link the production of a product to the production of another product—the amount of carbon necessary to produce a ton of steel, for example. This factory would propose practicable goals and take responsibility for any necessary revisions over the course of their undertaking. The problems of the society of the future are seen principally through the lens of management (Chaulieu, *Socialism or Barbarism* No. 22).[6]

Communist society will have plenty of complex technical difficulties to resolve—only, these difficulties won't fall within the purview of any particular authority. There's no point in trying to predict the forms that human activity will take, only in determining its content. There will be no unifying or managing what won't have been divided. The individual producer will see as much to his own activity as to its connection with the system of

---

6   This paragraph summarizes some of Pierre Chaulieu's proposals for a worker-managed socialist economy in "Sur le contenu du socialisme" [On the substance of socialism], in *Socialisme ou Barbarie* no. 22 (July–September 1957): 1–47.

general possibilities and needs.

In revolutionary society, relations between men and between groups of producers will be simple and transparent. The fear of competition that compels secrecy will cease to exist. It isn't important that each person arrive at *the universal science* and that each brain be a scaled-down "plan factory." What's the use of knowing where the ore in my fork came from! What matters is that the necessary information should circulate and be accessible.

In a fluid society where parochial attitudes and corporate patriotism have vanished, where each person can have many skills and play many roles, individuals and groups will orient themselves in accordance with society's needs.

Social obligations won't be imposed from without by some central office's intermediary, whether dictatorial committee or democratic assembly. The individual or group won't have to give way to their own awareness of circumstances, if we imagine this awareness as a simple reflection of external imperatives. People will act according to their awareness of social needs and possibilities, of course, but not in disregard of their own tastes. Often, there won't be any need for compromise. People feel their own desires as social needs before anything else. They're quite drawn to remedy things that they perceive as a lack. If I'm having trouble obtaining wine and I miss it, I wouldn't necessarily need to go look into production curves on a computer to know that maybe someone should go tend to the vineyards!

The communist man won't separate the pursuit of his desires from its social repercussions. He won't rush into tasks that are already being seen to. At any rate, it's stupid to think that the world will be made homogeneous and everybody will be carried away by crazes for the same activities.

Awareness of what's necessary to society will be much keener than it is now. All will be able to keep themselves informed, and capable of understanding what works and what doesn't, even if it doesn't bear direct consequences for each person. Computers will be indispensable tools for the circulation and interpretation of news.

The general organization of society doesn't necessitate a central govern-ing office, much less multiples of them. Perhaps there will be people who deal more specifically with gathering information and making plans, but they won't have blueprints to draft, in the imperative sense of the term. Planning amounts to the desire to shackle the future to the present!

Organizing can't become the work of any given caste. It'll be done constantly and at all levels of society. Men, no longer being divided by a thousand barriers, will coordinate as a matter of course.

Not everything will necessarily go smoothly. Some conflicts will be inev-itable. But the point of the revolution isn't to rid society of all conflict, nor to engender a society where everything will be harmonized a priori. Certain forms of conflict will, of course, be eliminated—those that divide classes, nations... But in the world that we want, opposition will have as much of a place as agreement. Harmony and balance will be forged by means of conflict and debate.

The fundamental difference with the current situation is that each person will only be bringing their own forces to their own battles. It'll no longer be possible to allude to abstract rights, detached from the tangible world of oppositions and power relations. It'll no longer be possible to win recognition for the legitimacy of a cause through recourse to specific bodies like the army or the police.

Communism will make conflict normal and even necessary, provided, of course, that the benefits at stake are no less than the damages caused. Capitalism is profoundly antagonistic. It's founded on the opposition between classes, nations, and individuals. Everyone's in opposition with everyone else. It's to ward off this reality that people preach fraternity and starry-eyed love. Aggression erupts everywhere, but the picture of peace must reign. Whenever people brutalize each other, it's not in the name of any individual interest but for the good of civilization, of universal values, etcetera etcetera.

Don't you risk wasting a lot of time in idle discussion and conflict? By addressing the problems of coordination and adjustment down at the level on which they actually arise, there's actually the chance of saving some time. But the idea that time is a thing that can be lost or saved is astonishing enough in and of itself.

From a communist point of view, the problem can't be reduced to knowing which method might conserve the most time. What matters is how this time is spent. Will people find it enjoyable and interesting to debate and come to agreements, or will they prefer to limit themselves to wordlessly implementing the resolutions of a governing committee that's planned in advance for a lack of conflict? Men will relearn how to talk to one another and have real debates in a considerate way. Tedious discussions will be limited by the boredom of their interlocutors, but also by the simple fact that everything won't always have to be brought back up. We'll be able to rely on past experiences.

Onerous jobs

There are some tasks that are indisputably onerous and unpleasant. We can hope to reduce them through mechanization, but someone will have to do them until then, and nobody can say whether all of it will necessarily be possible to eliminate.

It wouldn't be acceptable, and certainly wouldn't be accepted by the people involved, for those thankless jobs to lie on the same shoulders all the time. It'll therefore be necessary to arrange things so that the greatest possible number of people deal with them in rotation. The loss in profitability will be incidental.

In factories and other sites of production, people will easily be able to take turns at unpleasant positions.

At the level of society as a whole, people can call for these thankless jobs to likewise be subject to rotation. Everyone will be on garbage collection duty for some part of the year.

Onerous jobs are much less so when they're the extension of and pre-requisite for pleasant activities. Today, tasks are compartmentalized to an extreme, and the requirements of the "rational" use of the workforce demand that people do what they're qualified for while leaving the rest to others. In communist society, the researcher can very well deal with cleaning the facilities he uses, the motorist with helping tar the roads—and the dead with digging their own graves.

Unpleasant activities will be much less so when those who do them only give over a small portion of their time and no longer feel, as is currently the case, that they're shackled to them for life. Above all, these activities can be done in an environment that's entirely different from today—no more petty tyrants, no more obsession with productivity. Garbage collection, for example, could assume the air of Mardi Gras.

Many activities become onerous, not on account of their actual nature, but because they're made to be performed over and over again by the same people, and all in the name of workforce rationalization.

These transformations in the rhythm, the distribution, and the very nature of jobs obviously won't be planned in advance and pondered on high. They'll be made on the ground, in accordance with the wishes of the relevant people. If, on a construction site, there were someone passionate about wheelbarrowing or some other generally unpopular task, it would obviously be absurd to deprive him of his pleasure.

We aren't maniacs for equality. If there were a shortage of surgeons, it'd be idiotic to compel them to do the work of nursing assistants. That kind of inequality will only be mitigated by cultivating versatility and retraining people for sectors that are truly useful.

The end of separations

Communism signifies the end of the separations that compartmentalize our lives.

Professional life and emotional life are no longer at odds. There's no longer a time to consume and a time to produce. Schools, places of production, leisure centers—they're no longer distinct and mutually irrelevant universes. They gradually disappear with the disappearance of their specialized functions. Within the productive process, the hierarchization and segmentation of human activity fades away. This marks the end of those situations where the worker is the underling of the designer, the designer the underling of the engineer, the engineer the underling of finance and administration.

Bringing these changes to fruition will take some time. Our living environment—a specific variety of technological developments, habits, and human deficiencies—can't be wiped clean with the swipe of a dishcloth. It'll be vital to take active measures in this direction. Their effects will be felt the moment that commodity production and wage labor are abolished.

The separation between professional life, on one hand, and emotional and family life, on the other, is tied to the development of wage labor. The peasant saw himself torn from his land and his family so as to be integrated into the industrial sphere. Once, family constituted the unity of life and production. Husband and wife, but also children and the elderly, contributed to the work of farm and field. Each found useful activities that suited their strengths.

Reactionaries love to posture like defenders of the embattled family. These cretins refuse to see that the very order they defend is precisely what's reduced the family to the marginal role it's come to occupy today. The ties of kinship were ties of mutual aid, as far as farming went. They extended well beyond the couple and their direct descendants. Today, the family is nothing more than the production site for infants—if that! Its economic role is that of the unit of consumption. The fundamental institution, the baseline cell of the developed capitalist society, isn't the family. It's enterprise.

We don't intend to get the old patriarchal family back on its feet so that it can be made to handle production in lieu of capitalist enterprise. The ties of blood may have played a significant role in the past, but they no longer relate to much in the modern world.

In communist society, people will no longer be rounded up by the force of capital to carry out activities, productive or not. They'll bring themselves together, united by their shared tastes and affinities. The relationships between people will take on as much importance as production itself.

We aren't contending that strictly romantic ties will correspond to professional liaisons. That will be a matter of choice and of chance. But it'll be much likelier than it is at present.

Some people want to imagine communism as the communalizing of women and children. This is stupidity.

Romantic relationships will have no guarantee beyond love. Children will no longer be bound to their parents by the need to be fed. The sense of ownership over people will disappear in tandem with the sense of ownership over things. Now there's something deeply disturbing to those who can't imagine doing without the guarantee of policeman or priest. Marriage will disappear, in its capacity as state sacrament. The question of whether two (or three, or ten) people want to live together, and even bind themselves by pact, will be nobody's business but their own. We don't have to determine or limit in advance which forms of sexual relations are possible or desirable. Chastity itself isn't to be rejected. It's a perversion as commendable as any other! What matters, besides the pleasure and satisfaction of the partners, is that children grow up in an environment that meets their need for material and emotional security. That isn't a matter of morality.

In the remains of a family putrefied by the commodity, hypocrisy reigns supreme. People attribute to love what's nothing but economic, emotional, or sexual security. The relations between parents and children have reached the depths of degradation. Under the guise of affection, the will to exploit answers the desire to possess. The child carries the hopes of his parents' wasted lives like a millstone. He has to play the well-trained dog, succeed in school, show himself to be wise and calm or active and full of initiative. In exchange, he receives a bit of affection or pocket money.

Just as the family, that haven of security and love in a rough-and-tumble world, can't escape the commercial realities, the enterprise can't excuse itself from affectivity. The handshaking and seeming goodwill disguise contempt, rivalry, and exploitation. Everybody's lovely, everybody's sweet, everybody's chatting, but mostly, everybody's bored stiff of one another.

Production and consumption

The separation between production and consumption looks like a natural division between two very distinct spheres of social life. Nothing could be further from the truth. It's wrong on two counts.

Firstly: the boundary between what's called production time and consumption time is fluid, from an historical viewpoint, and vague, from an ideological viewpoint. In which categories do cooking and sports fall? It depends on whether they're undertaken by professionals or amateurs. It's not the nature of the activity itself that decides the question; cooking's more productive than mail sorting, in the sense that it's an act of material transformation, whether or not the cook earns a wage.

Many activities that once fell under consumption have moved into production. The astronaut and the invalid breathing oxygen out of tanks, the housewife buying ground coffee or canned goods—all participate in this shifting of boundaries.

The schism between production and consumption masks the continuing importance of unpaid housework in the modern world. It confers a fixed and natural appearance on a demarcation that's actually fluid and social.

Secondly: every act of production is necessarily also an act of consumption. People can only transform material in a certain way and to a certain purpose. At the same time that you destroy (or if you prefer, consume) something, you get (or if you prefer, produce) another out of it. Consumption produces, production consumes. Production and consumption are inseparable faces of the same coin.

The concepts of production and consumption aren't neutral. It can't be said that they're bourgeois, but bourgeois society has put them to specific use. A pear tree isn't bourgeois because it produces pear brandy. The notion of production takes on an ideological character because, beneath the idea of conception and detachment, people slip the idea of planning and consciousness. This maintains the confusion between the two. Everything ends up being interpreted in terms of production. A chicken becomes a factory for manufacturing eggs.

Thus is disguised the continuity of the cycle by which man, primitive or civilized, capitalist or communist, modifies the world around him by means that are simple or skillful, individual or collective, irreversible or temporary, at scale or in miniature—and, inseparably, is transformed in his own turn. The totalitarian usage of the notion of production hides the human being's radical integration in, and dependence on, his environment and its natural laws. Everything's interpreted in terms of domination and use. Man the producer, self-aware and self-controlled, sets out to conquer nature. The omnipotence that humanity once conferred on the image of the divine, it now attributes directly to the image it has of itself. Communism isn't the victory of consciousness over unconsciousness. It isn't the stage where, after having devoted himself to the production of things, man will finally be able to produce himself, so to speak, taking the reins from the divine creator. Hoping that man becomes his own master, the way he's the master of the things that he manufactures—this is hoping to reunite the separated under the sign of production, and therefore of separation itself. The producer wouldn't stop being an object; he'd simply become his own object.

The schism between production and consumption will fade because the separation between time spent earning money and time spent expending it—very tangible but very arbitrary, from the standpoint of nature and physiology—will cease to be.

For the communist man, consuming won't be opposed to producing, since there will be no conflict between caring for himself and caring for others. This is because, by producing for others, by exerting himself for others, he creates use values that he can help himself to as well. Nobody will be producing shoes in one moment so as to be obliged to go buy them at the market in the next. Above all, production will be transformed, becoming creation, poetry, expenditure. Groups and individuals will express themselves through what they do. In this, the revolution will be the proliferation of art, and art's advancement from its current capacity as a separate commercial sector.

Continuing to reason out the opposition between consumption and production, you could say that in finding satisfaction and pleasure (or, in counterpoint, dissatisfaction and displeasure) through his productive activity, man will thereby become a consumer. The computer or the trowel that he utilizes won't have a fundamentally different value from the car or the food that he makes use of at other times.

Communism is absolutely not production pressed at last into the service of the consumer, any more than capitalism might be a dictatorship of production. In devoting themselves to an activity, people will acquire a certain power. They'll be able to enjoy the fruits of their labor, up to a certain point, donating or refusing to donate what they produce. Above all, supplying this good or that service, and having them take a certain form, makes an immediate impact on what's possible in a society. The activity of the users will be determined by that of the producers. There'll be no reason for the latter to abuse a power which, in any case, won't be a political or a separate power, but the simple expression of the usefulness of their occupations.

The "consumer" won't be able to reproach the producer for some flaw, overlooked in pursuit of profit, in something that wasn't given in exchange; simply put, he'll critique the producer from the inside, not the outside. What's at stake will be their shared work, if they participate in the same enterprise. If someone's dissatisfied with something that was done or not done, he won't be able to evoke his abstract rights as a consumer. He'll have nothing to set forth but his own ability to do better, or at least to show off his own contributions. Criticism will be impassioned and constructive. It can't be left to those who are happy to make fun but prefer not to get involved.

Production and education

The separation between productive life on the one hand and education on the other isn't the fruit of necessity. It doesn't find its raison d'être in the growing scope of knowledge to be digested. Or rather, it does, but you then need to understand why it's become necessary that knowledge no longer be the direct fruit of experience.

The basis of this schism is that the proletarian can't be allowed to see to himself, his pleasure or his education, while he's producing. This separation, key to the survival of the economic world, comes at a very steep cost. It leads a significant portion of the population to stagnate in schools, vocational colleges, and universities, when they could be making themselves useful elsewhere and having more fun besides. It doesn't allow for human abilities to adapt very well to the demands of the activities they need to be applied to. This canned education is supplemented by on-the-job training, which is often done surreptitiously.

The school is presented like a public service that transcends social class. Its usefulness is supposed to be incontestable. Who'd have the nerve to become an apostle of ignorance? Enlightened minds do dare to go after the subject matter of instruction. They criticize it for being archaic, for being detached from life, for being a factor of subversion. Depending on whom you ask, toddlers should learn to read from the Holy Gospels, the *Communist Manifesto*, or the *Kama Sutra*!

Extremists are starting to go after the school itself. This isn't on account of its deadly efficiency but because of its inefficiency. They're going after the school in order to better protect pedagogy.

It's necessary to learn and to always be learning. To digest this insipid mush that people call culture. The world is so complex! You don't understand? Then you'll need to be retrained.

Never before have people learned so much; never before have they been so ignorant of the things that touch their own lives. They're inundated, dazed by the mass of information pouring out of universities, newspapers, television. The truth will never emerge from this accumulation of commodity-knowledge. It's a dead knowledge, incapable of understanding life because its fundamental nature is precisely that of being detached from practice and lived experience.

The school is the place where you learn reading, writing, and arithmetic. But the school is above all an apprenticeship in renunciation. There, you learn to bear boredom, to respect authority, to win out against your friends, to bluff, and to lie. There, you sacrifice the present on the altar of the future.

Communism is the decolonization of childhood. There will be no further need of any particular institution for educating children. Are you worrying about how children will learn to read? Then you should worry first about how they're learning to speak.

The school dissociates and inculcates the dissociation between the effort (or the learning) and its need. What matters is that the child should learn to read because it's necessary to learn to read, and not for the sake of satisfying his curiosity or his love of books. The paradoxical result is that, if it has reduced illiteracy, it has at the same time stifled most people's taste and true capacity for reading. In communist society, the child will learn to read and to write because he'll feel the need to learn and to express himself. The children's world not being separated from the rest of social life, learning will become a pressing necessity to the child. He'll do it as naturally as he learned to walk or talk. He won't be left entirely to his own devices to do so. He'll get hold of parents or elders, better informed than he is, to help him. The difficulties that he encounters will be useful to him. By overcoming them, he'll learn how to learn. By not receiving knowledge like predigested food from the hand of an educator, he'll acquire the habit of looking and listening; he'll become capable of developing understanding and making deductions on the basis of his experience. This will be lived experience's revenge on the curricular and extracurricular programming of human beings.

Men will share their experiences and transmit their knowledge amongst themselves. The places and the times will be chosen at their convenience. The format of the relation won't be determined a priori. It'll depend on the contents of the exchange and on the mutual understanding of those involved on the subject in question. With all due respect to fans of active pedagogy, if 10 or 10,000 people start waiting around to learn what a single individual knows, it'll become simplest to revive the lecture hall.

The modern interest in pedagogy reveals the fact that teaching methods aren't imposed on the basis of any particular content. When there's nothing left to be said, when the content of instruction has become interchangeable, then people discuss the way in which to say it. It's when the soup's bad that you take an interest in the appearance of the bowl.

What would happen in the world of capitalist production if workers suddenly had the right to truly experiment, no longer being judged on their immediate profitability? They'd very quickly be in danger of forgetting why they were hired. They'd derive experience through experimentation and experimentation through experience. Being unconcerned with production, they'd quickly be in danger of abandoning efficiency in pursuit of their own pleasures. The joy of discovery and the intoxication of freedom would replace routine and repetition. The connections that would be formed between workers, under the pretext of improving production through experimental exchange, would run the risk of taking a different direction. Why not give in to the heady joys of collective sabotage, why not organize games, why not reorganize or redirect production toward routes that directly benefit workers?

The principle of wage labor prohibits trusting workers to submit to the necessities of the production system—a production system that doesn't matter to them. Even the most alienated, hard-working, and servile of wage laborers couldn't be held back from this slippery slope. You can't let a worker make his own decisions during the production process. An instrument needs to be treated like an instrument. Let him look after himself and he'll acquire a taste for it, rising up against the capital that denies him his humanity.

The capitalist division between production and learning has its limits.

It's impossible to completely dissociate production, education, and experimentation. In production, even the stupidest job requires a certain adaptability from its worker, the ability to deal with unplanned situations. Likewise, in education, the greatest abstractions must be made tangible through certain "products," even if they're only exam books. The necessities of extrinsic testing fall back on production.

The student isn't a soft wax onto which knowledge can be imprinted; he can learn nothing if he stays completely passive. Learning can't completely absolve itself of experimentation and production, even if it sequesters itself from the actual economic sphere. The school serves to provide a restrictive setting and a content for this activity, to uncouple it from real life. Instruction functions and is perpetuated by means of the principles it represses. This applies to training in interpretation and composition. In this way, the latter becomes the very negation of communication. The student must learn to express himself in writing, regardless of what he might have to say and regardless of those to whom he might say it. It's a completely empty exercise. If the student manages to write, however, he was made to do so, and it was only possible by couching it in a certain form of communication. In the same way, the laborer who's made to work can only perform his work by participating in it up to a certain point. He's only ever a simple executor, a machine.

The system of production would collapse if workers could no longer experiment, help each other, advise each other. The hierarchical organization of work can only survive when its rules are constantly being flouted. It imposes an insurmountable boundary on these transgressions and on the spontaneous activity of workers, so as to prevent them from evolving and becoming truly dangerous and subversive.

TRACT II

5.

MONEY AND THE ESTIMATION OF COSTS

Communism is a world without money. But the disappearance of money doesn't mean the end of all estimations of cost. Human societies and actions—past, present, and future—are invariably forced to confront this problem whether or not they use monetary symbols. Depending on the underlying nature of a given society, the criteria chosen for these estimations obviously vary.

Money

In developed capitalist society, when the commodity is made the generic form for products, money presents itself to all the world as a necessity, even though not everybody might have the same amount nor make the same use of it. It's a good almost as necessary for human life and almost as natural as oxygen. Can anyone survive without money? Both rich and poor have to reach for their wallets to meet their most essential needs—or their most frivolous whims.

The objective though limited role occupied by currency corresponds to the subjective and fantastical role it occupies in the social consciousness. All wealth ends up being assimilated to monetary wealth by the servants of the economy. What can't be paid for seems to lose all value, even when it concerns the goods most vital to life: air, water, sun, spermatozoa, soap bubbles. Paradoxically, this era is coming to an end, albeit in the sense that the triumphant economy is hard at work assigning market values to everything, putting water in bottles and sperm in banks.

Where the common are content to note money's omnipresence and omnipotence, trying to make the most of favors from this capricious divinity, gentlemen economists take it upon themselves to defend it. Money isn't only vital in present-day society—a truth based on daily and, unfortunately, indisputable experience—it's vital to all social life that's even remotely civilized. Monetary circulation is to the social body what cardiovascular circulation is to the human body. The history of progress is the history of the progress of currency, from the seashell to the credit card. You want to rid society of money? You have to be mentally retarded, an advocate for the return to the barter system. (In passing, we'll note this about the much-disparaged barter: not only has capital not eliminated it, capital is constantly reinventing it, especially at the level of international trade.)

Currency becomes a veil that ends up obscuring economic reality. There are no more milling machines, no engineers, no spaghetti... only dollars and rubles. The illusion—that the control of currency, its issuance, its circulation, its distribution, corresponds to a comprehensive control over this collection of remaining use values—is imposed by the economy. Hence the disappointments.

Money's often pleasant, but what's responsible for that isn't so much its existence as it is the stinginess with which it creeps into people's pockets. The more it's criticized, the more it's demanded. If you want to smash the golden calf and root out idolatry, it's best, for efficiency's sake, to have a fat wallet; you can choose between the stupefaction of work, the danger of the stick-up, the vagaries of the lottery...

With all due respect to economists, money is a very strange thing. This becomes blindingly obvious as soon as you stop worrying about its undeniable economic usefulness in order to focus on its human usefulness.

Let's do our best to be naive.

How is it possible—by what infernal magic was it that wealth, the possibility of satisfying needs, came to be embodied in currency? If it had to take a particular form to remain visible to our eyes and remind us of its good offices, it could've followed the example of our Lord Jesus Christ and chosen bread and wine, which are good and useful things. But no! It preferred to manifest in the form of gold and sliver, metals that rank among the rarest and least useful. Worse, it no longer shows itself to mere mortals these days except in paper form.

The only need that currency meets is the need for exchange. It'll disappear with the disappearance of exchange.

It's monstrous to want to abolish money while preserving exchange or hoping for equal trade at last. At the beginning of the 19th century, "Ricardian socialists" proposed that commodities be directly exchanged in proportion to the amount of labor devoted to their production.[1] The Bolsheviks Bukharin and Preobrazhensky propagated similar delusions in 1919:

> Thus, from the very outset of the socialist revolution, money begins to lose its significance. All the nationalised undertakings ... will have a common counting-house, and will have no need of money for reciprocal purchases and sales. By degrees a moneyless system of account-keeping will come to prevail. Thanks to this, money will no longer have anything to do with one great sphere of the national economy. As far as the peasants are concerned, in their case likewise money will cease by degrees to have any importance, and the direct exchange of commodities will come to the front once more ... The gradual disappearance of money will likewise be promoted by the extensive issue of paper money by

---

1   This refers to John Francis Bray's idea of equal exchange between producers, meant to address the ills of rent-seeking and labor exploitation. Bray, *Labour's Wrongs and Labour's Remedy: Or, the Age of Might and the Age of Right* (Leeds, 1839), especially chapter 8, "The Requisites of a Social System," 108-120.

the State ... But the most forcible blow to the monetary system will be delivered by the introduction of budget-books and by the payment of the workers in kind ... (*The ABC of Communism*).[2]

There have been attempts to demonetize the economy, at least in part. Transactions between enterprises only exist as quantifiable operations. This hasn't produced anything worth noting nor anything very communist

Compliments

In the communist world, products will circulate without money needing to circulate in the opposite direction. Balance won't be achieved at the level of the household or the enterprise—what goes out in goods corresponding to what comes in, and vice versa. It'll be established directly, in a comprehensive way, and measured directly by the satisfaction of needs.

The end of exchange obviously doesn't mean that children will no longer be able to exchange their marbles and stickers, nor lovers their compliments. Limited bartering will persist on a small scale. Especially at the beginning, it'll supplement general distribution networks and find solutions for their inflexibilities.

The best indication that the secret of currency doesn't lie in its material nature is that monetary standards change depending on time and place. Salt and livestock were able to play that role; precious metals, especially gold, were in the end only selected for their very uselessness. In times of scarcity, gold can't be withdrawn from circulation in order to be eaten. When gold is withdrawn from circulation in order to be hoarded, or to serve as ornamentation, this is in accordance with its economic value. Some of its qualities,

---

2   Nikolai Bukharin and Yevgeni Preobrazhensky, *The ABC of Communism*, trans. Eden Paul and Cedar Paul (London: Communist Party of Great Britain, 1922), 334.

especially its distinctive rarity, made it prevail at a certain level of economic development. In the first faltering steps of the mercantile system, salt was able to serve as currency due to its very usefulness, and to the fact that it was concentrated in specific places. It was the ultimate object of circulation.

Today, currency is moving toward dematerialization. It's no longer guaranteed by the value of its material but by the banks and financial systems that control and manipulate it. It isn't ceasing to be a medium of exchange, but it is becoming an instrument, principally, at the service of capital. This allows for it to be optimally recouped and utilized to finance investments and extend credit to capital.

Wiping out currency doesn't mean burning banknotes or dissolving confiscated gold in acid. These measures may be necessary for symbolic and psychological reasons, in order to disrupt the system. They won't be enough. Currency will resurface in other forms if the need for and possibility of currency persist. Wheat, canned sardines, sugar—these can become means of exchange, and even of wages. "You do this work, you get ten kg of sugar that you can use to get meat, or alcohol, or a straw hat."

The problem, first of all, is that of the struggle for production, for organization, against shortages. Then there's the implementation of deterrents and restrictions, with regard to those seeking to exploit the transformative period and establish a black market. Gold and other precious metals will be requisitioned by the revolutionary authorities to eventually be... exchanged... for weapons or food with areas not yet controlled.

Currency is the expression of wealth, but of commodity wealth. It's not the direct satisfaction of needs, but the means to satisfy them. It's therefore also the barrier that separates individuals from their own needs.

Men's aspirations lie in the reflections of the things, the commodities, that face them. In this game, you can only be swindled. Wealth—genuine happiness—cannot be, and must remain an inaccessible mirage as a matter of publicity.

The law of value

Currency is used for exchange. But currency also signifies measurement. What currency measures in an exchange—the price of a commodity—originates outside of the sphere of exchange.

How is equilibrium struck, in the capitalist system, between what's produced and what's consumed? Between efforts expended and benefits procured? How is one choice established as more rational than another?

The problem is part and parcel of each specific commodity. They are at once use value and exchange value. Use value is the benefit they're supposed to provide. The consumer is supposed to appreciate it directly. Exchange value, which is expressed in the price, corresponds to the expense by which this benefit is compensated—for the buyer, monetary expenditure, but expenditure in labor first and foremost.

The price of a good is determined by forces that are exerted at the market level, by supply and demand. But beyond that, it references the costs of production, which are composed of the labor directly expended and the labor implicit in the materials used for production.

Thus is expressed, in each commodity, the need for financial equilibrium between expenditure and social gain, which is reflected in the need for the financial equilibrium of businesses and households—the need for equilibrium, but not the equilibrium itself! The price of a good corresponds only in a distorted way to the amount of real labor actually expended, or even to the amount of socially necessary labor. Equilibrium is achieved, not at the level of the particular commodity, but at that the level of the whole entire system. And there, that equilibrium is in fact a kind of disequilibrium.

Is the price of a commodity determined by the amount of labor it holds? Yes and no. Yes, because the price tends to vary according to gains in productivity, since a product that requires twice as much time as another risks costing twice as much, and since the overall mass of labor determines the overall value of commodities. No, because you can't establish a simple and imperative link between each commodity and the labor expended. This is due to the vagaries of the market. This is because if the price of a commodity were actually determined by the tangible labor expended, then the more productivity dipped, the more workers would idle, the more the commodity would hike in cost! In reality, those with higher cost-prices are penalized, not rewarded. The winners are those who save on the costs of production and labor. This is because price formation is affected by the profit rate's tendency to equalize.

What's become of the labor theory of value, passed down from the classical economists who said that labor determines the value of economic things?[3] This law is a general law that determines, through price formation, the general evolution of the system. Capital develops and allocates itself according to how much it can save in labor time. Like a river—even if its path isn't the shortest, even if it loses its bearings in backwaters, even if it makes detours—ultimately, it blindly conforms to its natural incline by eroding all obstacles along the way. Far from contradicting this tendency, the expected profit that leads the capitalist to invest here or there, to choose this technique or that machinery, is only the tortuous path along which the tendency is imposed on him

In the end, the theory of value demonstrates less the linkage between the commodity and its price on the one hand and creative labor on the other, than it does their dissociation. Labor becoming value means that the endeavor frees itself from labor and worker in order to become a satellite in economic space, where it can move around according to the rules it sees fit to follow. All commodities, having become autonomous and competitive, end up measuring themselves against each other through exchange and by means of currency. The theory of value, whose development is one with exchange and its hold on human activity, will disappear with communism.

What about the overall equilibrium between expenditures and revenues within the

---

3   Adam Smith (1723-90) and David Ricardo (1772-1823), most commonly cited as having first described the labor theory of value.

system? This equilibrium is a disequilibrium. From the standpoint of value, society produces more than it spends. The surplus builds up. Without this, capital wouldn't be capital.

Marx has shown that there exists a special commodity which has a knack for producing more value than its production requires. It explains why capital in motion increases itself, instead of staying the same from transaction to transaction. This commodity is labor power; its price, lower than the value it generates, is the wage. The difference is surplus value.

On what's falsely called the "job market," the worker sells not his labor but his ability to labor: a portion of his time. Labor isn't a commodity; it has no value. It's the foundation of value. Labor itself, says Engels, no more has value than gravity does weight.[4]

When capital leaves the sphere of circulation in order to enter the lair of the capitalist, it swells with the unpaid labor of the worker—all without the law of value being flouted, without profit arising from any fraud or breach in the rules of exchange. Each capital-commodity can be broken down into constant capital, which corresponds to the amortization of the materials and machines used; variable capital, which corresponds to wages; and surplus value, or added value, which corresponds to unpaid labor.

Money is the bearer of a profound mystification. It conceals the original nature of what expenditures actually generated the product. Behind wealth, even mercantile wealth, there is nature and human effort. Money seems to produce interest, to multiply. The only source of value—if it should be mercantile, and all the better for it—is labor.

Of course, the most servile of economists do accord labor a small role,

---

4   "It is not labour which has a value. As an activity which creates values it can no more have any special value than gravity can have any special weight ... It is not labour which is bought and sold as a commodity, but labour-*power*." Engels, "Preface to the First Edition," in Karl Marx, *Capital* vol. II, trans. Ernest Untermann (Chicago: Charles H. Kerr & Co., 1907), 27.

alongside capital and land, as a source of wealth. This doesn't do away with the mystification, however, even in part. It isn't labor as such that's accorded this favor; it's labor as the counterpart to the wage. It isn't money that's reduced to labor; on the contrary, it's labor that's reduced, by way of the wage, to money.

Free distribution[5]

From the disappearance of money in communist society, people are often tempted to conclude that there will be no more problems of cost to resolve, that it'll no longer be necessary to estimate the values of things. This is a fundamental error.

That a good or service would be free is one thing. That it would therefore cost nothing is another. The illusion stems directly from the workings of the market system. People are led to conflate cost and payment. They no longer see anything but the payment, the monetary expenditure. They forget the expenditure in effort and materials behind the product.

For capitalism as much as for communism, free distribution doesn't mean the absence of expenditure. The difference between free communist distribution and free capitalist distribution is that the latter is only free distribution in counterfeit. Payment isn't non-existent; it's simply deferred or displaced. The fact that school or advertisements might be free doesn't mean that they exist outside the market system, or that the consumer doesn't end up footing the bill. The free commodity is hugely perverse. It signifies compulsory or semi-compulsory consumption, the difficulty of

---

5   "Gratuité" is a concept with no direct English translation, sometimes neologized "costlessness," "gratisness," or even "free-of-chargeness." This translation opts for "free distribution" from here onward.

opting in or out of what's "offered."

In the new society, the costs of things will still need to be ascertained and, if necessary, calculated. Not out of a mania for accounting, nor to prevent fraud, which will have become pointless anyway. It'll be necessary to account for expenditures incurred in order to determine whether they were justified and to reduce them where possible. There will have to be measures to evaluate the positive or negative impacts that the satisfaction of a need, or the implementation of a project, will have on the built and natural environment.

A needle, a car—do they justify the time and the exertion devoted to their production, or the drawbacks associated with their use? Is it better to establish a production unit here, or there? Does this production justify depleting an already-limited stock of minerals? Matters can't be left to chance or intuition. It's easy to grasp that all of this will entail estimation, calculation, and projection.

If we preserve the notion of cost, so loaded with economism, this is because it's not simply a matter of choice and measurement, of an intellectual process, but of physical expenditure. Whatever technical level attained, there will be activities that cost more than others, tasks that are more grueling. Everything becoming easy and interchangeable would be a sad thing, and more alien to a communist society than to any other.

The commodity presents two faces: use value and exchange value. They appear to come under two irreducible orders:

1. Use value, utility, has to do with the qualitative. Users compare and assess what best suits them, an airplane or an orange. The choice cannot be independent of their situations and their tangible needs.
2. Exchange value has to do with the quantitative. Goods are all evaluated and ordered objectively, in function of a single standard, whether it comes to an airplane or to an orange.

Communism isn't so much a world where the use value is perpetuated, finally freed from the exchange value that leeches off of it, as it is a world where exchange value is denied and becomes use value once more. Advantage and disadvantage fall within the same order of things, and are no longer lumped together and separated back-to-back. Value ceases to be value in order to reappear as expenditure, tangible and diversified. There's no longer a single standard allowing for quantitative comparisons between all things, but rather tangible expenditures and labors, varyingly burdensome, which have to be taken into account. In ceasing to be the backbone of value, in ceasing to be unified by the process of exchange, labor ceases to be *labor*.

The bourgeois economy is double-entry economics. The bourgeois individual is not a man, he is a business. We want to destroy every business. We want to abolish double-entry economics and establish simple-entry economics, which history has known since the time the caveman went out to pick as many coconuts as he had companions in the cave, and he went out with nothing but his own two hands (Bordiga, *Property and Capital*).[6]

There will be free distribution because the "gift" will replace the sale. Those who perform one task or another, with either the aim of directly benefiting themselves or of being useful to others as well, will pay directly through their efforts exerted.

Is this really new? No, since even today, it'd never occur to anyone to charge the price of their saliva for a discussion or an argument. In conversation, people don't trade off specified speaking times or specified quotas of decibels; they strive to say what they have to say because they believe they have to say it. The interlocutor, or listener, owes you nothing in exchange for their attention. The hope of a response, the danger of being met with

---

6   Amadeo Bordiga, *Proprietà e Capitale* [Property and Capital] (Firenze: Editrice Iskra, 1980), 28.

incomprehension, with silence, with lies—they're part of the game. They're neither the expectation of payment nor the risk of the market. In everyday life, speech isn't a commodity, and speaking isn't work.

What still holds true today for speech, when it isn't recorded and broadcast as a commodity, will hold true tomorrow for all of production. The estimation of cost will no longer be distinct from the effort to be made. The prerequisite, the first step in the calculation, will be the impulse that leads to one activity or another. A book or a shoe will be as "free" as words can be today. The gift implies reciprocity to some extent, as speech calls for response, but this is no longer the anonymous and antagonistic process of exchange.

Working time

Since the outset of the 19th century, when the official economist of the English bourgeoisie, Ricardo, proclaimed that the value of a product depends on the amount of work necessary to its production, there has been no shortage of people demanding that the worker receive the full value of his product. Profit was morally condemned as theft. The problem of socialism was that of remuneration, of a fair remuneration.

One American communist, J. F. Bray, rises even higher. He sees equal exchange not as the solution but as a means of preparing the solution— which is the community of goods. A period of transition, where nobody receiving more than the value of his work can become very rich, turns out to be needful. From warehouses, each person will receive the equivalent, in various objects, of what he will have produced in some other form. Equilibrium will be maintained between production and consumption.[7]

---

7   John Francis Bray, *Labour's Wrongs and Labour's Remedy*, 124, 161. 180. Bray never

In *The Poverty of Philosophy*, Marx pays homage to Bray but criticizes him, too. Either exchange, even equal exchange, leads back to capitalism...

Mr. Bray does not see that this equalitarian relation, this *corrective ideal*, which he wishes to apply to the world is itself nothing but the reflection of the existing world, and that it is in consequence quite impossible to reconstitute society on a basis which is merely an embellished shadow. In proportion as this shadow becomes substance, it is seen that this substance, far from being the dreamed-of transfiguration, is nothing but the body of existing society.

...or we do away with exchange:

That which is today the result of capital and the competition of workers among themselves, will be tomorrow, if you cut off the relation between labour and capital, the effect of an understanding based on the relation of the sum of the productive forces to the sum of existing wants. But such an understanding is the condemnation of individual exchange...[8]

Without wanting to resort to exchange, some revolutionaries—Marx and Engels most of all—understood the society of the future's pressing need to resolve the problem of costs and their accounting. These revolutionaries sought a standard to estimate and compare expenditures.

Typically, the standard proposed has been the quantity of labor, this quantity being measured by time and sometimes graded by intensity. In this way, all of society's investments can be reduced to some expenditure of time. The orange and the airplane no longer correspond to a specific quantity of money, but to a given number of hours worked. Despite their

---

fully elaborated his vision for a "community of possessions" outside of how it might be partially implemented during this transitional phase.

8   Marx, *The Poverty of Philosophy*, 85, 84.

differences in character, they can be compared on the same scale.

This approach seems logical. What can there be in common, between different goods, if not the labor that they hold? That's where Marx set out from, in *Capital*, to reveal labor as the source of value. What other standard is there?

For our part, we haven't evoked a "beyond work" in order to then throw ourselves onto the measurement of working time, miserably, as soon as it comes to broaching harsh practical realities.

The theory of the measurement of goods or the projection of investments via the quantity of labor is false. It must be radically rejected. This isn't a case of a dispute over method, but of a fundamental problem that concerns the very nature of communism.

Measurement by labor remains economistic. It seeks the end of the law of value but doesn't see all that this implies. Capitalist society tends toward perpetuating itself while being freed of class division and exchange value!

The aim is to solve a problem presenting two sides. The first is that of workers' remuneration. The second, and more general, concerns the distribution of productive forces in the social sphere.

How to distribute consumer goods without money? How to fairly reward the worker in proportion to effort exerted?

On this subject, Marx returns in *The Critique of the Gotha Program* to Bray's point of view. He rids it of its troublesome aspects. In a transitional period where the principle "to each according to need" won't yet be possible to implement, remuneration will depend on effort exerted. It will depend on it, not be equal to it, because a part of what this work represents will have to go to a social fund, to be devoted to the production of production goods, to aid for invalids... The worker can't receive the full product of his labor. Moreover, as there won't be any vouchers circulating to certify the amount of labor the worker has exerted, exchange will be nipped in the bud.

This means—this demands—that accounts be kept. "... Labor, to serve as a measure, must be defined by its duration or intensity, otherwise it ceases to be a standard of measurement."[9]

For Marx, the problem of remuneration is incidental and limited to the lower phase of communism. On the contrary, the question of the distribution productive forces is fundamental and permanent. In a communist society,

... the money-capital would be entirely eliminated, and with it the disguises which it carries into the [economic] transactions. The question is then simply reduced to the problem that society must calculate beforehand how much labor, means of production, and means of subsistence it can utilize without injury for such lines of activity as, for instance, the building of railroads, which do not furnish any means of production or subsistence, or any useful thing for a long time, a year or more, while they require labor, and means of production and subsistence out of the annual social production.[10]

Calculating the amount of necessary labor, however, doesn't mean that the law of value should be able to continue while money-capital disappears. In fact, the amount of labor is allocated according to need. In *The Poverty of Philosophy*, Marx writes:

In a future society, where the antagonism of classes will have ceased, where there will no longer be classes, use will no longer be determined by the *minimum* time of production; but the time of social production which will be devoted to the various objects will be determined by their degree of social utility.[11]

9   Marx, "Critique of the Gotha Program" in *Marx/Engels Selected Works* vol. 3 (Moscow: Progress Publishers, 1970), 18. No attributed translator.

10   Marx, *Capital* vol. 2, 361-62.

11   Marx, *The Poverty of Philosophy*, 68.

The law of value is only a particular, mercantile expression of a more general rule that is applicable to every society:

> Indeed, no form of society can prevent the working time at the disposal of society from regulating production one way or another. So long, however, as this regulation is accomplished not by the direct and conscious control of society over its working time – which is possible only with common ownership – but by the movement of commodity prices, things remain as you have already quite aptly described them in the *Deutsch-Französische Jahrbücher* ... [12]

That's what Marx wrote to Engels, 8 Jan. 1868. What was the thesis that the latter had expounded?

> As long ago as 1844 I stated that the ... balancing of useful effects and expenditure of labour on making decisions concerning production was all that would be left, in a communist society, of the politico-economic concept of value. ... The scientific justification for this statement, however, as can be seen, was made possible only by Marx's *Capital* (*Anti-Dühring*).[13]

What Marx and Engels tell us about communist society—and you see that they talk about it!—flows directly from their analysis of capitalist society. Their conceptions are indebted to it for their strong suits, but also their weaknesses.

The strong suits are in showing that the problems of the distribution of consumption, of the remuneration of work, aren't fundamental. It's the

---

12 Marx to Engels, 8 January 1868, in *Karl Marx and Frederick Engels: Selected Correspondence*, ed. S, Ryazanskaya, trans. I. Lasker (Moscow: Progress Publishers, 1965), 199.

13 Engels, *Anti-Dühring, Herr Eugen Dühring's Revolution in Science*, trans. Emile Burns (Moscow: Progress Publishers, 1977), part 3, chap. 4, 340n.

mode of production that determines the mode of distribution. To assert that the laborer won't be able to receive the full value of his product, his labor—in opposition to the bleeding hearts—directly extends an analysis of capitalism that shows that the value of a commodity covers constant capital in addition to wages and surplus value. It's necessary to produce the instruments of production.

Capitalism and communism are tooled societies, unlike previous societies. Capitalism and communism are also changeable societies. You can't count on experience immemorial. Not everything is settled in advance by past custom, eventually amended by common sense. The estimation of cost isn't so much a problem of accounting after the fact as it is a problem of projection. There will rather be a regression, on this fundamental point, among the post-Marx communists. Some council communists will reduce the question to that of the truest possible snapshot of reality and economic movements.

The following passage shows how, for Marx, the current society and the society to come must settle the *same* problem, the first using money-capital—credit—and the second by doing without it:

However, on the basis of capitalist production, extensive operations of a long duration require large advances of money-capital for a long time. Production in such spheres is, therefore, dependent on the limits within which the individual capitalist has money-capital at his disposal. This barrier is broken down by the credit system and associations, connected with it, for instance, stock companies. Disturbances in the money-market, therefore, set such businesses out of action, while they, on the other hand cause disturbances in the money-market themselves ...

On the basis of capitalist production, it must be ascertained, on what scale those operations which withdraw labor and means of production from it for a long time without furnishing in return any useful product, can be carried on without injuring those lines of production which do not only withdraw continually, or at several intervals, labor-power and means of production from it, but also supply it with means of subsistence and of production. Under social or capitalist production, the laborers in lines with short working periods will always withdraw products only for a short time without giving any products in return; while lines of business with long working periods withdraw products for a long time without any returns. This circumstance, then, is due to the material conditions of the respective labor process, not to its social form.[14]

Marx and Engels go too far in situating communism as an extension of capitalism. That's what their shortcoming is.

They maintain the bourgeois separation between the sphere of production and the sphere of consumption. Already, the *Manifesto* distinguishes between the collective ownership of the means of production and the personal appropriation of consumer goods. It swears up and down that it only wants to socialize property that's already social and communal—the instruments of capitalist production. The *Critique of the Gotha Program* continues in pitting individual and family consumption, proportional to working time, against productive and social consumption. It doesn't linger over how to manage the latter..

There's been confusion around the distribution methods for products and their nature as "consumer goods" or instruments of production. On the one hand, there are individuals, and on the other, society as abstract conception. There are individuals—isolated, in a group, in communities—who face each other and organize.

In reality, when the state, or the head of the company, disappears in its capacity as representative of the "public interest," the Society as opposed

---

to the Individual disappears. There's no longer anything but men, isolated, in a group, in communities, who organize this way or that. An individual might be allocated a machining tool, or a neighborhood committee a few tons of potatoes.

The separation between the workforce—separate individuals—on the one hand, and social and collective capital on the other, disappears. It's not possible to maintain by invoking the need for remuneration during the transitional period. On the contrary, in Bray or Marx, it's the defense of this need that reflects the limits of an era, the immaturity of their communism.

Despite his vital and pertinent remarks, Marx remains dominated by the fetishism of time. Either he renders it an instrument of economic measurement or he renders it an instrument of super-economic measurement: "For real wealth is the developed productive power of all individuals. The measure of wealth is then not any longer, in any way, labour time, but rather disposable time."[15]

Working time is the basis of free time. The rule of freedom can only be founded on the rule of necessity.

The mistake isn't in continuing to envisage necessity, sacrifice, and production within the new society. The mistake is in bundling all of this together, slapping it with the label "working time" (to be reduced, if possible) and universally pitting it against free time.

In *The Critique of the Gotha Program*, Marx says that labor will one day become the first among needs. This formula didn't fail to be exploited, in a foul way, by Stalinist leaders. In any case, there's a contradiction there. Does labor, in communist society, become expenditure or gratification? Is it necessary, consequently, to reduce working time to a minimum or, to the contrary, to produce as much labor as possible in order to satisfy those calling for it? It's only in a capitalist society that work could appear as the

---

15   Marx, *Grundrisse*, trans. Martin Nicholaus (London: New Left Review, 1973), 708.

first among needs, as the only means of satisfying the others. It's only there that it can be hated and clamored for at the same time.

Fantastical

It's a pretty fantastical thing, measurement by working time.

Wanting to measure all productive activities by the time they necessitate is like wanting to measure and compare all liquids by their volume alone. Of course all activities take some amount of time, just like all liquids occupy some amount of volume. That isn't completely unimportant. A liter water bottle could also contain a liter of wine. But who'd go so far as to deduce that a bottle of water is therefore always equivalent to a bottle of wine, of alcohol, of grenadine syrup, of hydrochloric acid? That could only make sense, in a pinch, from the restricted perspective of someone who warehouses them.

Time is the only language that can express the creative efforts of the serf or the worker from the perspective of the exploiter. This signifies external measurement, surveillance, and antagonism. The duration and intensity of the activity win out against its specific nature and arduousness, which tend to become irrelevant. The subjectivity of experience is sacrificed in favor of the objectivity of measurement. Creation and life are subordinated to production and repetition.

Measurement by time predates the mercantile system. The exploited, in lieu of providing some number or another of some product or another, place a certain portion of their time at the disposal of the exploiter. See the corvée labor of feudal times. The procedure was remarkably developed in the Incan system. That was a great agrarian empire, unified by a bureaucracy, where money was unknown. Services were made in the form of working days spent in this or that domain. It led to meticulous bookkeeping.

In communities of peasants or villagers, you spend a day harvesting at your neighbor's, and vice versa. The peasant and the blacksmith trade their products on the basis of production time. The activity of a child is reckoned as some portion of that of an adult. You can see, in these practices, the origins of using time as a universal standard, and even of subjugating the planet to the market economy—but only the origins. With these marginal practices, it's more about mutual aid than exchange. The activities measured are of the same nature, or comparable in concrete terms. Measurement by time isn't independent of the matter measured.

It's with the dual development of the market system and the division of labor that measurement by time has begun to take on its fantastical character. It detaches itself gradually from the matter of activity as the latter is diversified.

This process escalates when exchange infiltrates the sphere of production. Measurement by time develops in conjunction with the tendency to economize working time. The greatest possible amount has to be produced in the shortest possible time. This prospect, measurement by time, isn't independent of human activity's compression into the smallest possible temporal volume. Not only does labor produce the commodity, the commodity produces labor through the intermediary of factory despotism.

In doing so, measurement by time no longer appears in its innocence; it's veiled behind money and justified by financial necessities.

Bourgeois ideologues, especially those who align themselves with Saint Marx, project this fetishism for time and production onto all of human history. It's no longer anything but a constant struggle to free up time. If savages have remained savages it's because, restrained by their feeble productivity, they never found the time necessary for the accumulation of a surplus. Time is scarce; it has to be packed, as densely as possible, with activity.

But far from thinking exclusively about how to save time, savages are rather concerned with the most effective means of squandering it. They're often of a nonchalant nature. Other than a few hunting implements, they're little concerned with accumulating goods.

In the 18th century, Adam Smith gave up on basing value on working time, as far as modern times are concerned. But he did see this labor-value at work in primitive societies where things haven't yet gotten so complicated.

He imagines hunters wanting to exchange their assorted game. *What basis can they do it on, if not on the basis of working time, depending on the time needed to catch the animals?* This presupposes an economist and mercantile mentality in an environment where rules of sharing and bonds of reciprocity prevail.

Let's assume, however, that trade already exists, or that our savages have decided to expend their energy rationally so as acquire meat at the lowest cost. Will they establish their system on necessary labor time?

There are pleasures and risks with hunting, about which the time spent on it divulges nothing. Where's the value in a comparison based on the length of the hunt, regardless of the difference in risk, between lion and antelope? Some hunting methods may be less swift but more certain, less exhausting, less dangerous, more or less cruel.

If they nevertheless wanted to continue practicing this method of measurement, could they do so? It's very difficult to assess the time it takes to overcome this game or that with any precision. By systematically hunting the most profitable meat, from this narrow point of view, you'd quickly risk changing the conditions and the time required for the hunt. In any case, people very often go hunting deer and bring back rabbit. Useless to plan for what can't be planned.

Are we going to be told that this no longer holds true for our civilized and enlightened era, that the hunt is a very specific productive activity? Let's set the record straight. It's the ubiquity of exchange that conceals the truth from us. Measurement by working time doesn't transcend hazards, human risks, the depletion of resources. These problems don't belong only to savages but to all society. Repressed by the logic of capital, they return with a vengeance.

Measurement by time only indirectly accounts for the onerousness of the activity and its repercussions on the environment. With communism, could it be used in translating the modification or destruction of a landscape—the depletion of a mine, the oxygen production of a forest—into a communist language? A production's incidental advantages and disadvantages might be assessed in terms of working time potentially saved or potentially spent. This would be outstripping capitalism in absurdity, by openly and consciously seeking to reduce use values and occupations to labor-values. How to evaluate the value of a landscape? Do you have to consider the expense required to meticulously reconstruct it? At that price, not much would be profitable.

In assessing the different values of two equal durations of work, in which the risks and onerousness were different, would it be right to compare them on the same scale? An hour of masonry might cost the same as an hour and a half of carpentry. You'd either assess that the difference corresponds to the expenditure in time necessary to tend to the mason, to wash his clothes... or you'd give up on reducing everything to an expenditure of labor time. But then how to determine the coefficients quantifying the differences of value and onerousness that lie between tasks? For that matter, why seek to determine objective coefficients when these differences depend on conditions, and on the pace of the activity, and on the tastes of the participants?

Let the workers unshackle themselves, and the proponents of measurement by time, or remuneration according to hours worked, run the risk of being left behind. As soon as activity ceases to be compressed, it'll change nature and expand. The quantity and character of a production will no longer be possible to evaluate in terms of some duration of labor consumed. Someone who only sticks around for a short time might still produce enough; another might spend their entire day there doing hardly anything. If remuneration is meant to be based on time in attendance, it'll call for tireless prison guards or it'll quickly become an invitation to laziness.

Whether workers reach an agreement in order to ensure a specific output, or to devote a specific number of hours per day to productive tasks—that's a question of practical organization, not directly linked to determining the costs of what they produce. One factory could spend twice as much time as another to fabricate objects of identical cost.

You can certainly talk about the social distribution of the working time that a community has at its disposal. But you can't forget that time isn't some substance that can be slopped out with a ladle. It's men who will go to this place or that, who will take care of this task or that. From the moment that free time stops being exceptionally scarce and reserved for meeting absolutely necessary needs, there will be some tasks more urgent than others, some men more rushed than others.

With capital, it's necessary to dissociate price, the expenditure of labor power, and what it brings about: labor that has no value. With communism, this dissociation loses its meaning. It's no longer possible to partition the labor power from the labor, the man from his activity.

This means that surplus value no longer exists, first of all, even monopolized for the community or in some new form of social surplus. People can no longer talk about accumulation nor about growth, except regarding physical size. To talk about socialist accumulation is an absurdity, even if at some point people produce more steel or bananas than before, even if people devote more social time to production. These moves no longer translate into value, or even into time expended.

This then means that labor, which has no value within capitalism, takes on value within communism. This value that it takes on is neither moral nor mercantile. It doesn't mean eulogizing labor but expressing, on the contrary, its transcendence.

Labor, the source of value, is a constant. It can be economized, but its identity is never in question. With communism, a given activity will no longer be distinguishable from the trouble of the people who do it. Not all undertakings bear the same human cost. It's a matter of cultivating the least costly ones.

Labor also has a cost in capitalist society, if you abandon the perspective of capital for that of the worker. Some jobs are preferable to such or such other jobs. In the evening, you feel your fatigue and your annoyance.

But ultimately, the differences are faint, work always being considered as time more or less wasted. People don't bother to calculate boredom, or the degradation of health. For the worker, the price of all this shit is his wages. People know that it's all a hoax, and that wages aren't determined by effort expended or boredom experienced.

The superiority of communism is that it doesn't satisfy itself with satisfying the needs of "consumption." It tackles the transformation of productive activities—the conditions of labor, if you prefer. Investment decisions aren't made primarily as a function of working time saved, even if the speed of execution made possible could play a part in reducing it.

It's a matter of privileging the activities that are most pleasant by producing the conditions under which activities take place. Determining the conditions of activities doesn't mean determining the activities or the behavior of the producers themselves. The producer stays in control of his actions, but he acts within specific conditions, according to specific constraints within which he can act.

The production of instruments and of the plans of production, by men, allow for this transformation of human activity. The development of technology can be oriented in a direction more or less favorable to the producers. This or that type of machine, or ensemble of machines, allow those who use them to wear themselves out less, to be less at the mercy of production speed. It's possible to systematically develop the conditions that allow men to be as free as possible within the production process.

Let no one tell us that personal tastes or subjectivity inhibit objective thinking about all choices. There exist general constants. We aren't then claiming that criteria must be of universal scale. They vary according to time and according to situation. Men will organize themselves to determine what's best. Differences in taste and a willingness to experiment can lead to them to develop differing approaches toward the same goals.

The estimation of costs can't be reduced to the necessity of bringing "revenues and expenses" into equilibrium. The equilibrium has to be conceived of as a dynamic equilibrium. Starting from the conditions left behind by capitalism, it becomes a question of guiding a certain kind of development. Does the agreed-upon cost for constructing some productive outfit, some living environment, justify itself? Does the automation of some unit of production justify the efforts necessary to the manufacture of automated machinery? The logic of economizing working time, which in the capitalist world organizes the development of circumstances, cedes its place to a different logic—a logic that's no longer external to the men who put it in practice. Humanity organizes and controls the structure of circumstances according to its needs. In this sense, it becomes situationist.

Elevator or stairs?

Behind the economic notion of cost, we have to track down the most ordinary and banal reality that it ends up concealing.

Everybody asks themselves the question of whether or not what they're doing is worth the trouble. Does the expected result justify the expense and the risk? Are there less costly, which is to say more agreeable, ways to obtain a similar or sufficiently satisfactory result?

If this genre of question fell under the jurisdiction of economics, the world would be nothing but economists and managers. In reality, these are economic and financial problems that are a specific and rather bizarre case of a more general problematic.

Spontaneous and naive evaluations of cost long preceded the advent of capitalism. It persists, marginal to the economic sphere, even though our choices must constantly account for financial necessities. What characterizes it is that it's done without monetary detours, and that it isn't reduced to criteria of time.

At its outer limits, the evaluation of costs isn't the preserve of humankind. The pigeon that hesitates to come peck at the seeds you offer it is, in its own way, giving the thing a try. The fact that it misjudges the risks and ends up in a stew changes nothing about the business. Estimation doesn't necessarily rule out error.

The bird's choice has more to do with instinct and habituation than anything else. With human beings, it moves to a different level.

The individual who finds himself at the foot of a building—who has to get to a certain floor, who has the choice between elevator and stairs—finds himself confronted with a problem of cost. Maybe he'll hang around pondering for an hour, maybe he'll make his choice automatically without even considering it.

The problem is simple, if reduced to the three solutions on offer: elevator, stairs, or leaving altogether. It becomes complicated if you take into consideration the elements that take part, consciously or not, in the decision-making. What floor does he need to get to? Does he even know? Our man, is he in good health? Old? Tired? Legless? What's the height of the steps? The steepness of the stairs? The speed and the frequency of the elevator? The urgency of his gait?

The decision made will not be economic. It'll be subjective, direct, and bound to a tangible situation. It isn't monetary. It's not a matter of knowing which solution will cost the most, provided that the elevator doesn't cost money like they sometimes do, and given that someone's already paid for its operation anyway. Speed of execution might take part in the choice—it could maybe become decisive—but that's not relevant to the situation. Time savings will prevail if, by some misfortune, we've come across a firefighter. Maybe he'd prefer to use his truck ladder anyway.

How to apply to the economy that which is rightly external to the economic sphere? This is a fake problem. The real problem is precisely whether or not it's possible to go beyond the economy, to dissolve it in its capacity as a separate sphere.

It's a question of doing away with the economy. This didn't become possible because we suddenly discovered that you can replace current methods with processes that are simpler and more direct. Paradoxically, it's the development of the economy—the socialization of production, the astounding interdependence of businesses, the development of economic forecasting and calculation methods—that make this rupture possible.

Going forward, the principles that guide our choices will be as simple and transparent as the ones we live by all the time. It'll be a matter of reducing effort, trouble, expenses. That won't be the goal for social life in and of itself, but it'll be a tendency at the heart of, and in accordance with, all projects implemented. Maybe people will set themselves very difficult and very perilous tasks, but they'll do their best to make them easier. A team of mountaineers can set out to conquer a tough summit without agreeing to do it with their bare hands.

Simple principles don't always mean easy methods and solutions. Difficulties will arise from the complexity and the very nature of the problems to be solved. Maybe they'll also spring from a calculation method's inadequacy to the object of calculation, or from the difficulty of determining selection criteria. The risk of error, the necessity of being content with approximations—these condemn nothing. In any case, it wouldn't constitute a step backward with regard to the present stage.

What today applies to the use of stairs versus elevators will tomorrow apply to their production and their installation. The objective constraints within which the user navigates will no longer be determined economically.

Is it better to build a stairway, an elevator, both, or nothing at all? These questions imply a whole series of others. Is this need so important and so frequent that it justifies the expense necessary to creating the stairway, the elevator, the rope, or the kick in the ass that lets you to get to the desired floor? The perspective can be reversed. Should tall buildings be constructed, given the cost of elevators? On the contrary, given the pleasure provided by this manufacture of elevators, should we build more skyscrapers?

The list of questions to be posed is practically infinite. That seems daunting. In reality, only a limited number will ever be posed. Many are ruled out by simple common sense. Our mountaineers won't be able to demand an elevator for their expedition. Every decision is made within a tangible situation where a whole host of questions have been settled, a priori, by the facts. Force of habit plays tricks on us, but it also spares us trouble. There's every chance that the man who was at the foot of the building based his decision on it. The estimation of costs assumes its full importance when people find themselves faced with a new situation, when people initiate a new production process. The problem of manufacturing and installing the elevator or the stairway is likely to be a widespread problem, carried out according to known elements. Any case that's a bit particular or a bit new will be treated as a modification of a more classic situation.

There exists a hierarchization of solutions. When you decide to start construction on a building, the cost of a means of ascent—approximately known—will probably be secondary. Once the general decision is made, it'll become necessary to construct the stairway, the elevator, or both. The choices that remain will concern the nature and quality of the materials. These choices still won't be made in absolute terms but according to the products and the techniques actually favored and developed in that field. Every choice aims to draw out the optimal solution, but every choice is made in accordance with some number of constraints. The optimum itself is likely to be a compromise between the interests of the different groups concerned.

Ending the division of the economy into competing enterprises doesn't mean that all social production will form into nothing more than a single coordinated body, where all activity would be immediately subjugated by another, where there would only be one sole common interest, and where the estimation of costs would be made at a global level. For reasons human and technical, producers will divide themselves into groups whose opinions may diverge but whose interests will no longer be at odds. Even if individuals move from one occupation to another, one workshop or construction site to another, even if groups aren't permanent, division in time and space will persist.

The construction of a building entails the mobilization of varying trades. You can imagine that, under communism, the architect would become a laborer, mason or painter. This won't preclude the division of men into distinct teams and work into separate phases, especially if it's a major construction. Builders will have no choice but to call on outside input. They may need to get assistance or advice. Above all, they'll need to procure themselves machines and materials.

The products sourced from without—how to figure out and account for their costs? Builders can try to make the task easier for themselves, when it comes to the distribution and employment of their own resources and abilities. But when they have to draw on stocks they haven't amassed themselves, this is no longer the case. A material that's easier to use, or that'll bring more satisfaction to the building's users, might nevertheless be rejected given its manufacturing cost. In each situation, in order to avoid waste, the benefit gained must justify the expense.

Products, and even implementation processes, need to have an objectively known cost. It's on the basis of this cost that users will make rational choices.

Does this mean that each product will bear a label on which its "price" will be written? Will a housewife doing her "shopping" find herself faced with cabbages or carrots accompanied by a quantitative index?

That would be a sad replication of the current situation. As a general rule, each person will take what he needs the moment it becomes available, as long as he isn't aware of any need more urgent than his own. The calculation of costs is first and foremost a projection, and it's directly manifest in the nature and quantity of goods offered. No need for a quantitative label to exert pressure, if not on the wallet, then at least on the intentions of the user.

There are various types of cement that presently have, and will certainly continue to have, varying costs of production. It'd be stupid to use a cement that's twice as expensive as another one that would work. Generally, the visible nature of a product, or the accompanying user manual, suffices to determine its proper use. It'll suffice to specify in the user manual, when there's a risk of confusion, the differences in cost between different products.

Currently, dead labor weighs on living labor, the past on the present. With communism, the cost of a product isn't the expression of value to be realized, of equipment to be amortized. This means that an object's cost won't necessarily represent the expenditure it required—or even an average of the expenditure required for all products of its variety.

A product will be allocated by the cost at which it can currently be replaced. A hike or a drop in productivity wouldn't have any reason to translate into a difference between production costs and selling price. It would immediately be recorded as such, including for already-manufactured objects. This variation may result in the expansion of the production concerned if it becomes more profitable. The augmentation of investments won't have surplus profit as its basis.

There might be cost differences in the production of the same product or of two similar products. These differences might arise from the continued use of some manufacturing processes more outdated than others. Often, they'd be determined by natural conditions. Agricultural yields are highly variable; not all mines are equally easy to exploit. Does this mean that similar products will be affected by different costs, or that an average price will materialize, applicable to everything, the way that average market prices tend to materialize today?

It'll be very important that differences in cost be known, but this won't impact the users of these products. There will be no advantages for some and disadvantages for others. It's simply a matter of developing the most advantageous manufacturing processes.

If an escalation in some production signifies a drop in profitability, this doesn't mean that it should necessarily be ruled out. First, because this drop in profitability might be a brief and passing phenomenon. Next, because it's necessary to judge the importance of the needs to be met. As with regard to the production of food, an escalation often means diminishing returns: people cultivate less-fertile lands. This is no reason for refusing to feed some portion of the population and launching into activities whose profitability is on the rise.

Returns might only diminish in the short term, anyway. Sowing in a desert isn't very promising, but very significant investments—implementations of irrigation processes and new cultivation methods—could change a lot of things. Some sun-baked desert once irrigated, some marine farm, could very well win out over traditionally fertile lands.

What seems impracticable today will be possible tomorrow. Modern technologies, instead of fueling the arms race, will serve to fertilize the deserts.

From the moment that the demand for a good increases, it's likely to lead to a drop or a hike in the cost of producing new units. A drop will tend to increase demand for that product. If there's a hike, on the other hand, it'll be a matter of knowing when costs start becoming prohibitive. In this case, it'd be necessary to determine whether it's the latest demand that should be diverted or, on the contrary, if it should be satisfied by abandoning or reducing other demands.

Calculation

From the moment of tackling the implementation of complex productions or projects, when some decisions determine a succession of other decisions, it becomes necessary to be able to forecast and calculate in order to select the least costly processes. Cost must often be estimated based on the long term. A momentary gain, or a lack of research, could have costly consequences for future prospects.

In choosing one or another track gauge for a railway, you're committing in a way that can only be reversed with some difficulty. In this case, as in many others, a lack of foresight at the outset can lead to much less rational operating conditions down the road.

It's a matter, also, of determining the technical coefficients that interconnect the productions of different products. The production of some material or some object necessarily involves the production and expenses of other goods, following some defined ratio.

It's a matter of anticipating possible expenses, of simulating a project's culmination. These forecasts can pertain to projects that are significant for the resources they mobilize, for the duration of their roll-out, for the hazards they entail.

Let's assume that some men have the ambition to reach, explore, and eventually settle on a virgin planet. Such an operation can't be launched into on the spur of the moment. It's necessary to evaluate the possibilities and anticipate costs.

The first evaluation of the affair's soundness will be presented by the number of individuals who agree to support or participate in it. This number will be itself determined by the impression of seriousness conveyed by the project and its advocates.

Once the project's initiated, it'll be necessary to make choices, and make these choices compatible with each other. Should exploration be focused on automated vehicles or on manned vessels? Should these vessels opt for an atmosphere of air or of oxygen?

Today, these are technical questions freighted by financial and political constraints. With communism, there's no longer anything but technical questions that are also human questions. The debate over automated vehicles, manned or mannable, bears on the level of science, on the comfort meant to be provided to the cosmonauts, on the construction effort, on the prospects of each project...

The options chosen influence each other. However, not everything needs to be decided and planned for in advance. The first decisions guide what's to follow, though without defining everything in detail. What matters is that at each stage, the best option possible is chosen, and that it doesn't lead to a dead end. The number of decisions to be settled is enormous, but they wouldn't all be settled at once, and corrections can be made.

Why further complicate life with all these issues? With capitalism, all of that's resolved automatically.

Nothing could be further from the truth. Just because costs become monetary prices, and the market sanctions the behavior of businesses, doesn't mean that everything is automated. Planning and projection exist on a general level, and this also applies to businesses of even the slightest consequence.

Not all operations are immediately sanctioned by the market. Such sanctions represent the final step in a system of expenditures and decisions.

If possible, it's important to anticipate the market's decisions. Powerful businesses no longer base their prices on market fluctuations, but aim to calculate then impose an optimal price. This price isn't necessarily the one that will allow them to move the most goods, or even to maximize short-term fiscal returns. It can be set according to an overall strategy. In the Eastern European countries, prices are beginning to be determined by mathematical means.

In the East, as in the West, businesses are tending to cut themselves loose from the market in order to impose their strategies through their prices. It's not an entirely new tendency. It's intensifying, today, through the power of corporate groups, through the technical possibilities of individualizing products, through the development of the methods of economic calculation. Competition and the market haven't been abolished. Their effects have simply been deferred, and the struggle between monopolies isn't directly and solely fought out on the level of prices.

The important thing is that, at the very heart of capitalist society and businesses, methods of assessment and projection are being developed that can be used in a more systematic way with communism. The development of computers has been accompanied by a whole body of mathematical research aimed at representing and theorizing reality in order to address problems of choice, of simulation, of economic strategy. Even when it stops being a matter of best appraising and meeting financial criteria, it'll be possible to use and expand on this research.

By current custom, businesses don't count on the market to organize the production of goods as rationally as possible. The market presents one sanction for behavior, but not a precise and technical guide for that behavior.

Thus, let us imagine an industrialist who would like to manufacture, using sheet metal, the maximum number of cylindrical cans. If he's partnered with an engineer, he will be able to immediately calculate the height/diameter ratio that ensures the best use of the metal; this ratio is equal to 1.103. If not, our industrialist will adopt values "at random." But if some competition arises between several enterprises, those that have chosen the poorest values will be ruined. And so, through purely experimental means, manufacturers will be driven to retain—without knowing why—coefficients ever closer to 1.103 (*The Book of Life*, A. Ducrocq).[16]

"Scientific" rationalization extends to the very organization of production and distribution. Operations research supplements custom and common sense.

As early as 1776, the mathematician Monge undertook to systematically study the least costly methods of excavation and backfill.[17] This also led to purely mathematical discoveries. Applied to military operations during the Second World War, operations research has continued to develop thanks

16   Albert Ducrocq, *Le roman de la vie, cybernétique et univers II* [The Book of Life, Cybernetics and the Universe II] (Paris: René Julliard, 1966), 184.

17   Gaspard Monge, *Mémoire sur la théorie des déblais et des remblais* [Thesis on the theory of excavation and backfill] (Paris, 1781).

to the power of electronic calculators. It's used on problems of competition and reaction between adversaries; the phenomena of waiting; inventory management; projections of wear and replacement for equipment; simulation; etc. It's no longer a simple matter of accounting, but of deduction on the basis of the analysis of past and present, of what may come about and what would be most desirable.

Comparisons

With communism, just as with capitalism, it's important to be able to compare in order to estimate costs and choose the best solutions. But how to compare?

It's all simple so long as there's currency, which is to say a universal equivalent, since any good is supposed to be possible to evaluate according to this single standard. There's a quantitative ratio between all products. But when people decide to do without currency, or even measurement by quantity of labor, what can comparison be based on? What else can be found that's common to all goods, that can facilitate comparison between them?

There's no other single, universally applicable standard. We'll therefore do without one. This won't prevent comparison. These comparisons will be qualitative, and founded on varying and variable criteria. They'll no longer be carried out in reference to some abstract and universal model. They'll stay connected to their concrete circumstances and objectives.

The fantastical thing is that different goods can be made equivalent to each other, regardless of their particular natures. It's understandable that foodstuffs can be compared according to their protein content, their weight, their freshness. But these varying criteria don't allow for the denotation of some general equivalence.

The need for a general equivalence can't be dissociated from the need for exchange. All things must be possible to compare, from a universal perspective, because they've become tradable goods, economic values. This is precisely what needs to disappear, and what the dream—or the nightmare—of measurement by labor time would seek to disguise in order to save.

Even under the reign of capital, not all comparisons can be reduced to comparisons of value. Goods are still use values. The buyer's judgment focuses on price, but also on the product's usefulness and quality.

When a housewife does her shopping and chooses between a head of lettuce or a bunch of radishes, she does so according to the tastes of her son-in-law, the previous day's meal, the look of the produce, the space remaining in her basket... Price is really only the deciding factor when two identical products have different values.

The multiplicity of criteria that come into play don't prevent the housewife from making comparisons or choices. Her judgment is subjective. It isn't universally valid. This doesn't mean that it's irrational, relative to the situation at hand.

When it comes to choosing between several manufacturing processes, it of course becomes necessary to reach a more general consensus. The choice will be less subjective, in the sense that it must be disentangled from momentary dispositions, and in the sense that it'll have longer-term consequences.

Currently, purely monetary evaluations are occasionally inconclusive or overridden by other evaluations. Political necessities, and the dangers of significant fluctuations in certain prices over time, thwart financial prospects.

Let's take up the issue of nuclear power plants. Besides the economic arguments, there are opposing viewpoints on the ecological, social, and political costs. There's talk, often in bad faith, of energy efficiency, of the problems of transporting and storing waste, of national sovereignty, of the creation or destruction of jobs.

In communist society, it's no longer necessary to render all comparisons on a universal scale. It's sufficient to be able to determine the possibilities actually present, and to promote those that give the fastest results, those that are the surest, the least dangerous...

The important thing is to determine a set of pertinent criteria as you go along, and, in accordance with these criteria, to directly compare the conceivable solutions against each other. It's not so much a question of quantifying as of sorting and ordering criteria and solutions. It's the relative, qualitative meaning that predominates.

We aren't counting on calculators to sort everything out. But they'll be necessary and utilizable:

> Initially designed for accounting operations and a posteriori management, employed also for scientific calculations, they have long been considered (ten years, maybe...) as tools intended to furnish quantitative results. How this characteristic is changing. Thanks to the methods of operations research, and more specifically to those of simulation, the accumulation of figures have brought about a qualitative result: one is no longer interested in exact numbers but in their relative meanings, on which the orientation of choice depends. Thus do calculators become means of forward-looking management (*Operations Research*, Faure, Boss, and Le Garff).[18]

What needs to be simplified and universalized aren't so much the decision-making factors at play as they are procedures for resolution, the programs that will allow whole sets of data to be processed. In a certain sense, the more important the number of criteria, the more precise the representation of reality tends to be.

You can imagine what would come of a debate on the priority to be

---

18   Robert Faure, Jean-Paul Boss, and Andre le Garff, *La recherche operationnelle* [Operations Research] (Paris: Presses Universitaires de France, 1961), 125-126.

accorded to different sources of energy. A significant number of data would come into play. You couldn't go off of just one criterion without admitting some perversion of reality. Choices need to be made in a comprehensive way, in accordance with broad factors, but also in a localized way, in accordance with the resources and needs of varying regions.

Communism doesn't rule out choices and comparisons that are purely quantitative. These remain valid when a single criterion for selection suffices, depending on the nature of the products at play. This is the case when it comes to increasing or reducing a given production. This is the case when a savings in expenditures corresponds to a quantitative savings in the use of a material devoted to the same use, as in the case of canned foods. But even here, this savings must not be considered as a savings in working time, but simply in the amount of materials. That it should translate into a reduction in the duration of productive activity—this is simply one possible consequence.

Shouldn't we be concerned about this communist frenzy for rationalization? Doesn't it run the risk of catching up to the capitalist frenzy for exploitation?

Today, rationalization and exploitation are conflated. Man tends to be considered an object that needs to be squeezed for as much as possible. Inhumane methods, having nothing to do with technical constraints, are developed: hellish production rates, double and triple working shifts. Capitalist rationalizations, whether brutal or gentle, are more or less always carried out against men. That's why it always stays fundamentally irrational.

Communist rationalization doesn't aim to impose a pace on work. By nature, it will tend toward augmenting the liberty and the satisfaction of human beings. Decision-making and implementation won't be made externally from the tastes and habits of the people involved. There will be technical constraints, production needs that will influence the speed and duration of activities. But this will no longer have anything to do with rendering human capital profitable.

6.

BEYOND THE POLITICAL

Communism isn't a political movement. It's the critique of the state and of politics.

The intention of revolutionaries isn't to conquer the state and help themselves to its power, clad in the ulterior motive of destroying it. The party of communism doesn't claim to be a political party and it doesn't mean to compete with these bodies.

With the establishment of communist community disappears all political activity, in its capacity as a distinct activity, and all pursuit of power for the sake of power. There is no longer a divide between the economy, that sphere of necessity, and politics, that sphere of liberty.

The end of the state

The cult of the state is fundamentally anti-communist.

Paradoxically, it's born of and strengthened by all the flaws, all the failings, all the conflicts that capitalist society engenders. It is the supreme savior—the last resort of the widow and the orphan. Incidentally, although it claims to be above class, presenting itself as the public interest's protector from individual excesses, it busies itself with defending property and privilege.

There was a time when the ascendant bourgeoisie exhibited anti-state sentiments. Today it only sulks. The time of bourgeois revolutionaries, claiming that the happiest peoples are stateless peoples, is over. The rise of the proletarian peril, the development of competing imperialisms, the sweep of economic crises—they've demonstrated all the benefits of holding a powerful machine of state and, above all, a good apparatus of repression.

In the name of the people, political parties vie for mastery of this state machine that they present as a neutral instrument. Logical Leninists proclaim the classed nature of the state and the impossibility of controlling it through simple electoral victories. They deduce from this the necessity of its dismantlement, but only in order to replace it with a "workers' state."

It's to the anarchists' credit that they've maintained a fundamental anti-statism.

However, even more than with the case of money, everybody makes it their duty to curse the state. They rail against the red tape of the administration, the burden of the taxes, the arrogance of the police, the graspings of politicians, the stupidity of voters... But the disappearance of the state—that's what exceeds the limits of the imagination. And this is the very thing that they propose, unimaginatively, to bring to power.

Over the last few decades, the state has intervened more and more openly in social life. The advents of Stalinism and fascism were only the most visibly-marked stages in this process. Where some have imagined seeing the state making concessions to the people, it's necessary to see the escalation of state control over their populations.

Especially noteworthy is the taking in hand, or the integration into the state apparatus, of organizations for workers' defense and solidarity. Through various channels, social security and the apparatuses of trade unions have been subjugated to the state. This allows them to act more or less as special-interest groups. You can't be deceived by their declarations of independence and opposition. It's written into their roles.

Obviously, this assimilation of the struggle and officialization of the social partner have been presented as great victories for the working class. Workers' struggles benefit a stratum of contestation specialists and result in the increased institutionalization of "workers'" organizations. Often, these "gains" don't even result in a redistribution of resources to the most disadvantaged social strata, only helping to squeeze them for even more money—despite what's claimed, hypocritically, by unions and governments.

Growing nationalization can't be considered solely as a weakening of the proletariat. On the contrary, it corresponds to the necessity of controlling the proletariat's growing power. This nationalization compensates for the fragility of modern societies. But it isn't itself immune to that fragility; the state enclosure of the population is only possible with the complicity of that population. The anti-political revolution will ultimately reveal the superficial nature of this enclosure.

Unlike politicos of every persuasion, revolutionaries refrain from appealing to the responsibility of the state as soon as some problem arises. They systematically forward the autonomy and self-organization of the proletarian class. Invoking the weakness of the proletariat in order to justify recourse to the state—that justifies the weakness and poses it as eternal.

Revolutionary society will have systems for coordination and centralization. Often, it will even enable a more advanced, more global centralization than that enabled by capital. But it will have no need of a state where power is concentrated, of all this machinery for repressing, identifying, surveilling, educating. The administration of *things* will replace the government of *men*.

During an insurrectionary and intermediate phase, the problem is to avoid recreating a state while safeguarding functions that are administrative and repressive—and thus state-like. Those who don't want to deal with this problem, like anarchists, can only be cuckolded by statists or forced to become statists themselves. During the Spanish Revolution, the participation of anarchist ministers in the junta government demonstrated what this could lead to.

The solution to this problem, to this contradiction, has been outlined by proletarian insurrections since the Paris Commune. It's the workers' council, the councilist organization of social life.

Workers' councils

The Paris Commune had already offered the first glimpses at what a government of workers could be.

In 1905, insurgent Russian workers elaborated the form of the *soviet*. This organ, composed of factory delegates, was initially intended to coordinate the struggle. It transformed, bit by bit, into an administrative body aimed at taking the place of the official administration. The Petrograd Soviet even brought a portion of the police force under its control. Its existence came to an end when tsarist forces arrested its deputies. In 1917, with greater participation from soldiers, it began anew. The Bolshevik coup d'etat of October 1917 happened in the name of the power of the soviets. It relied on the soviets of Petrograd and Moscow, where Bolsheviks were controlling the military commissions and had conquered the majority of votes. This victory was the beginning of the end. With the waning of the revolution—the civil war, the fortification of the party and the administration of the Bolsheviks—the soviets were progressively emptied of their substance. The final resistance of the soviet, at the Kronstadt naval base, was crushed in 1921 by a Red Army directed by Trotsky, erstwhile president of the Petrograd soviet.

The proletarian uprisings of the 20th century regularly brought about the resurgence of the soviet system. In the wake of the First World War and the Russian Revolution, workers' councils were formed in Hungary, in Germany, in Italy, The Spanish Civil War would see the proliferation of committees of workers and peasants. In Hungary, in 1956, factory delegates formed the Central Workers Council of Greater Budapest. In Poland, in 1971, insurgent workers of the Baltic ports once again organized themselves on this model.

The word *council* actually includes fairly diverse forms of organization, even if you exclude those organizations for co-management or management that aren't at all revolutionary. This ranges from the committee for a factory, or a neighborhood, to the soviet that runs a large city or region. It's a mistake to try to pit these organizations against each other in order to confer the title of "workers' council" on only some of them.

We aren't for this or that specific form of council. We're for the councilist organization of society. This entails and necessitates varying levels of organization that complement and support each other. What would be bad—and what has regularly happened—is if one level were to win out.

The factory committee can be reduced to a simple function of worker control or pure management of a production unit. The lack of actual soviets in Spain and Catalonia, despite the flourishing of rank-and-file committees, left the field open to the Republican state and its politicians. Hence the anarchist dilemma.

The soviet, cut off from its rank and file, can turn itself into a kind of regional state or workers' parliament. It ceases to be an active and anti-political organ so as to become a battlefield of political parties.

What gives the workers' council its revolutionary character, what gives it its anti-political content, is principally the fact that it's the direct embodiment of the masses in action. It's formed of a pyramid of committees, giving rise to one another without the top being able to believe itself independent of the base.

The committees aren't simple electoral assemblies, delegated power from the bottom up. Each level fulfills practical functions. Each committee is a community in action. It delegates to the higher levels what it can't resolve on its own. It doesn't surrender its sovereignty. Delegates are accountable to their mandators; they are accountable and revocable.

The workers' council doesn't reproduce, within itself, the divisions between legislative, executive, and judicial powers. It is concerned with unifying and concentrating, under its direction, these varying functions. Even if it issues decrees, it acts first and foremost in accordance with the circumstances without taking refuge behind an arsenal of formal laws.

The workers' council establishes itself as a tribunal in order to settle conflicts—in order to judge, decide, and punish. These actions are carried out in accordance with concrete situations. What's judged isn't the gravity of the wrongdoing; it's the damages and objective risks for the revolution and society.

The council doesn't see its legitimacy secured by democratic elections that would render it the people's anointed. It isn't the representative of the masses. It is the masses, organized. Individuals and groups that take responsibility for particular tasks aren't necessarily elected. But when they embroil the whole council, they're responsible before its general assemblies. The council doesn't claim to be the embodiment of all society, above the conflicts that society faces. It's an organ of class and struggle. This implies some minimum of agreement, at its heart. It can't tolerate divisions that would paralyze it.

The workers' council can be viewed as an ultra-dictatorial or an ultra-democratic form. It's both of these and something else besides. It's ultra-dictatorial in the sense that it doesn't purport to be accountable to anything but itself, and that it runs roughshod over the sacrosanct principle of the division of power. It's ultra-democratic in the sense that it enables the masses to debate and participate to a degree never attained by the most democratic of states.

Above all, the workers' council is no longer a political organ. It no longer partitions the citizen from the social individual. In this, it's beyond dictatorship or democracy, which are the two faces of politics—even if it still makes use of processes or forms that are democratic or dictatorial.

The council is neither the instrument of a popular democracy nor the instrument of a dictatorship of the proletariat. These expressions don't manage to characterize the phase of rupture between capitalism and communism.

The workers' councils of the past, apart from a few rare instances, fell well short of the program that we're tracing. They were managerial, bureaucratic, pedantic, argumentative, dispute-ridden, incapable of holding a perspective consistent with their own natures. They died of it. This doesn't prove that the councilist form is worthless, but rather that it was founded on ground that wasn't yet fertile.

In 1956 the Central Workers Council of Greater Budapest, which governed the entirety of the region, called for its own suicide with the restoration of parliamentary democracy.

The workers' councils of the past nevertheless have the merit of having existed. They demonstrated the capacity of workers to see to their own affairs, to take charge of and run their own factories and towns. They're linked to the formidable movements by which workers toppled the bourgeoisie and the bureaucracy, at least for a while. If these episodes have been concealed and confused, it's because some people don't want to see the proletariat once again resuming what it did in Catalonia, in Poland, in China: to do without masters and be fine for it.

The counterrevolution, including in the Soviet Union, has never been able to accommodate this. That the councils demonstrate moderation is one thing; that the counterrevolution be moderate toward them is another.

The workers' councils' best showings have taken place when they've had to respond to their enemies quickly, clearly, and forcefully. They're forged directly as an organization of struggle. Their project may be limited, but they know it.

At other times, they get bogged down in administration, in waiting. Their sole raison d'être seems to be the bourgeois power vacuum. You see the development of magnificent organizational structures—but this is carried out in the void, outside of the imperatives of struggle. The apparent absence of peril leads to the worst delusions.

The council appears as a worker response to the vacuum left by bourgeoisie, rather than as a level of organization imposed by the radical nature of the struggle itself.

We are for workers' councils. But we are against councilist ideology. This ideology sees councils not as a moment in the revolution but as its goal. Socialism is the replacement of the power of the bourgeoisie with the power of the councils, of capitalist management with worker management. The failure or the victory of the revolution is a matter of organization. Where Leninists put everything on the party, councilists put everything on the council.

Workers' councils will be what they do. Their only chance of victory is to undertake—and to be—the organization of communization.

For communists, revolution isn't a matter of organization. What determines the possibility of communism is a certain level of development of the productive forces and of the proletarian class. There are problems of organization, but they can't be posed independent of what's actually being organized, the tasks actually being set. Are organizational rules neutral? Are they purely technical questions? Of course not. Their determinations are of great importance. Some complement and foster communist action. Others impede it. But it's a serious delusion to believe that the promotion of certain rules, especially on the control of delegates, would be enough to prevent bureaucratization, lies, division. Bureaucrats are professionals of the organization in its capacity as a separate organization. They like to stress the prerequisites of action, the democratic mechanisms, rather than action itself. Frustrating and ill-suited rules, even if they're formally anti-bureaucratic, run the risk of expediting the task.

In the event that councils do develop and can no longer be easily liquidated, the worst enemies of the revolution will pretend at being councilists in order to best put an end to councils. They'll try to turn them into arenas for their own machinations, to exclude revolutionaries. Against communism, the dregs of the old world won't hesitate to rechristen themselves as councils.

From the character of past councils, often not very communist, can it be deduced that the time for councils has passed? Isn't all institutionalization counter-revolutionary?

We don't see workers' councils as institutions. Like it or not, the revolution will have to deal with problems of administration, of maintaining order, of integrating opposing tendencies. It'll still be necessary to govern, if not all people, then at least some people. Looting can be considered a healthy reaction to scarcity and the provocations of the commodity. It might play a beneficial role in a phase of rupture: sinking the commodity and letting off steam. But you can't institutionalize looting by making it the regular method for the communist distribution of products. Products can't all be left up to unrestricted distribution. It's necessary to organize, allocate, limit. That's the task of the councils.

As the scarcity of goods begins to ease and the counter-revolution to retreat, councils will lose their state-like character. They won't be retired. They'll blend into social life.

To reject councils out of purism when they arise in accordance with real needs is to cut yourself out of the revolutionary process. It's better to participate in their creation, in their operation, in their potential dissolution, depending on the struggle and the balance of power between revolution and counterrevolution.

Participation in councils doesn't signify that revolutionaries have to renounce acting and organizing autonomously. Councils are mass organizations—hence a certain ponderousness, hence a pace of radicalization slower than that of some segments of the population. The evolution of councils will be partly determined by what's done alongside them.

What needs to be combated and sabotaged are the corporatist councils, the managerial organizations, the neo-syndicalist or neo-political groups that would seek to appropriate the organization of social life for the benefit of a minority. A system can't be called a soviet if it would preserve commodity production, build up a police force, demand the return of bosses...

The council is necessary when it comes to administering a territory. They vanish when this necessity disappears temporarily, in relation to some balance of power, or permanently, due to the consolidation of communism. Some groups might intervene and communize stocks of goods, depending on a revolutionary situation, without being willing or able to permanently take on the attendant production and distribution. The question is knowing when people have the means to move on, from this type of ad hoc wildcat action, to the direct administration of a territory. The advantage is that they can better manage their resources in order to feed the population or lead the struggle. The disadvantage is that they paint targets on their backs. From the moment they accept this risk, there arises the problem of the councilist organization of the territory—the problem of the constitution of a revolutionary power.

Even if this power needs to seek the greatest support and participation from the masses, it doesn't seek to establish itself democratically, for example by organizing elections.

Democracy

What is there beneath the heavens more beautiful than democracy, the power of the sovereign people? The term *democracy* inspires as much support as *capitalism* can arouse distaste. Everybody's for democracy, whether they be republican or in a crown, bourgeois or for the people. If there's one thing everyone scolds their adversaries about, it's that they aren't democratic enough.

Anyone who rises up against democracy can only be nostalgic for the absolute monarchies of old, at best. In general, people preferable to slap them with the infamous label of fascist. The most dogged are often Marxists and Marxist-Leninists who forget what their founding fathers said about democracy, who are eager to mask their own taste for power and dictatorship... Hypocritically, certain guilt-ridden nostalgics of Stalinism will accuse us of being Stalinists.

Democracy seems like the antithesis of capitalist despotism. Where everyone knows that a minority rules in actuality, they claim to oppose it with the power drawn from universal suffrage.

In reality, capitalism and democracy are in league. Democracy is capital's fig leaf. Democratic values, far from being subversive, are the idealized expression of the actual, less-than-noble tendencies of capitalist society. Communists don't intend to realize the trinity "liberty, equality, fraternity," any more than "work, family, fatherland."[1]

If democracy is the daughter of capital, how is it that dictatorship and capitalism should so often coexist? How is it that the majority of men live should under authoritarian regimes? How is it that, even in democratic countries, its workings should be constantly disrupted?

Democratic values and aspirations are the consequence of capital's homogenizing nature. They correspond to the end of the individual's integration into a community and a network of stable relationships. They also correspond to the necessity of maintaining an idealized community, of resolving conflicts, of limiting clashes for the good of all. The minority yields to the majority. Democracy isn't a simple lie, a commonplace illusion. It draws its content from a torn social reality that it makes a show of reunifying. Within democratic aspirations, there's a search for community, a will to respect the other. But the basis on which it takes root and tries to grow prevents it from succeeding.

Still, democracy is often too dangerous for capital, or at least for certain established interests. This is why it's constantly being subjected to constraints. Apart from a few exceptions, these constraints, and even simple dictatorship, are presented as victories for democracy itself. What tyrant doesn't claim to govern, if not through the people, then at least for the people?

Democracy, which during calm periods can seem like a good way of paying off workers' struggles, sees itself shamelessly abandoned as soon as

---

1   "Liberté, égalité, fraternité" [Liberty, equality, fraternity] has been the motto of France, more or less officially, since the Revolution. During World War II, the Nazi-collaborationist Vichy regime replaced it with "Travail, famille, patrie" [Work, family, fatherland].

the defense of capital demands it. There are always a few intellectuals and politicians entirely surprised to see themselves so readily sacrificed upon the altar of the interests of the powerful.

Democracy and dictatorship oppose each other, but they aren't alien to each other. Democracy, as far as it implies the minority's subjugation to the majority, is a form of dictatorship. To make decisions, a junta of dictators does have to resort to democratic mechanisms.

It's sometimes forgotten that fascism, Nazism, and Stalinism, in order to establish themselves, mingled terrorist tactics with regular elections. They enjoyed pitting the broad masses, their popular tribunals, against handfuls of "traitors," "anti-patriots," the "anti-party."

Communism isn't the enemy of democracy because it would rather be the friend of dictatorship and fascism. It's the enemy of democracy because it's the enemy of politics. That said, communists aren't indifferent to the regimes under which they live. They prefer to go quietly to sleep each night without wondering if this is the night that someone will come to drag them out of bed and march them to prison.

Critique of the state cannot replace critique of politics. Some attack the machinery of state only to better protect politics, just as some pedagogues critique the school in order to apply pedagogy to all forms of social relation. For Leninists, everything is political. Behind every manifestation of capital, they see an intention, a design. Capital becomes the instrument of a political project which must be opposed by another political project.

Politics is the domain of liberty—of action, of the maneuver—in contrast with economic fatalism. The economy, the domain of production and goods, is ruled by necessity. Economic evolutions and crises appear in the guise as natural phenomena that elude man's grasp.

The left is in the habit of emphasizing politics' possibilities, the right the necessities of the economy. A false debate.

More and more, politics is looking like a replica of economic life.

For a time, it was able to play a role of compromise and alliance between social strata. Today, the importance of politics as economic intervention has augmented. But at the same time, the political sphere has lost its autonomy. There's no longer anything but a single politic of capital, which both the left and the right are forced to undertake, regardless of the particular interests of their social bases.

If the state seems like a more-or-less delimitable institution, politics is born and reborn from every pore of society. Even though it manifests as the actions of a particular social stratum of militants and politicians, it's drawn from and reflected in the behavior of each person. That's what gives it its strength, what gives rise to the idea that any social solution can only be political.

Politics stems from—hinges on—the dissociation between decision and action, as well as on the separations that set individuals against one another. Politics appear primarily as this constant quest for power that animates men in capitalist society. Democracy and despotism themselves seem to be the only ways to resolve problems between people. Democracy's introduction to relations between couples, or families, passes for a new stage in human progress. Above all, maybe in the least unpleasant way, democracy suggests the loss of a profound unity that could unite human beings.

Communism doesn't separate decision and execution. There's no longer a division between two groups, or even two distinct and hierarchical moments. People do what they have to do, or what they've decided to do, without second-guessing about whether they're the majority or the minority—notions that presuppose the existence of a formal community.

The principle of unanimity prevails, in the sense that those who do something are initially in agreement, and that the agreement would have furnished the basis of and possibility for common action. The group doesn't exist independent of or prior to action. It doesn't divide itself up in the vote in order to then reunify through the subjugation of one party to another party. It's established in and through the ability of people to identify with and understand the perspective of the other.

It's not about systematically rejecting every vote and every submission of the minority to the majority. These are technical formations that can't be given an absolute value. It may be that the minority is the one in possession of the facts. It may be that the majority yields to the minority, given the weight of what's at stake for that minority.

Is it that communism is the advent of freedom? Yes, if by that you mean that men will have more choices than at present, that they'll be able to live in harmony with their preferences.

What we reject is the philosophy that brings free will into opposition with determinism. This separation reflects the opposition between man and world, individual and society. It expresses the deracination of the individual, his inability to grasp his own needs and to satisfy them. He can choose between a thousand jobs, a thousand hobbies, a thousand lovers, and be influenced in a thousand ways, because nothing actually affects him. No certainty occupies him. He doubts everything, himself first and foremost. In doing so, he's ready to endure anything, and he often believes himself to have chosen. Liberty presents itself as the philosophical garments of misery, doubt as the expression of free thinking when it actually signifies man's confusion, his inability to situate himself within the world.

Man loses his chains in the course of the revolution, but finally becoming himself, he finds himself enchained simultaneously to his desires and to the necessities of the moment. He once again becomes passionate, once again comes to know himself. The extraordinary climate of joy and of tension, in the insurrections, is bound to the feeling that everything is possible and, jointly, that what you're doing must absolutely be done. There's no longer any need to hesitate or be shuffled around between meaningless activities. Obligations, subjective and objective, blend together.

The electoral circus

If you attack democracy, the wise ones will counter us, it's because you know that it would doom you.

We're under no illusions. Were the system functioning normally, we'd absolutely be pulverized. Our platform might not be considered unsympathetic by most voters, but it'd certainly be deemed unrealizable. It's only by negating themselves as voters that they could begin to glimpse the possibility of its realization.

If politics is the art of the possible, as they say, we situate ourselves outside of that particular possibility.

Gentlemen electioneers and democrats, are you ready to question the population on certain issues and take their responses into account? You who are the lackeys of capital—are you ready to organize a referendum on whether or not to continue upholding capitalism? There are a multitude of questions that you'll make sure never to ask. They're ruled out from the start as unrealistic. It's you who determine what is and isn't possible. This still isn't enough for you. It's necessary that your realistic programs and your realistic forecast should never be implemented.

The state survives on the taxes of its citizens. It's managed through their voting. If its policies were to be approved and supported directly by private individuals' acceptance or refusal of tax payments, it would be in danger of losing many supporters. When he pays, the citizen feels a sense of having been had. When he votes—he who'd otherwise have to shut up—he's flattered to be solicited for his opinion.

There's a disconnect between, on the one hand, the actual management of the system and the classes of functionaries in charge of it, and, on the other hand, party politics. Political theater.

Electoral democracy serves to hide the fact that the important decisions are beyond the reach of voters and even politicians.

Political and electoral reality is more and more soused in the commodity.

Democracy appears as the direct reflection of the economic world. The voter is no longer even a citizen but a consumer of platforms and ideologies. The spectacle of politics and its privileged moments, elections, must be denounced for what they are: one way, among others, to make the people forget that they are nothing.

It sometimes happens that people take liars at their words. After witnessing annulled elections or what appears to them like an electoral victory, they start to rebel. This no longer has anything to do with electoral reality.

We don't advocate for electoral participation, and even less for abstention. When proletarians vote they are, if not right, then at least within their rights. This ritual will only really appear illusory, ridiculous, and pitiful when the whole of living conditions begins to truly transform. Meanwhile, it has its place with the rest of the arsenal.

In a communist organization, there may well be elections. That's how delegates are appointed. But the election no longer seems like a special moment. The elected no longer has a blank check. He fulfills a function that's one among many, and no more sacred than any other. In appointing this or that person or this or that team, or in approving their actions after the fact, the rank-and-file group is only providing itself with guarantees as to the implementation of its own platform. What counts isn't the procedure of appointment but the action really taken.

The formation of workers' councils isn't predicated on a general electoral referendum. It's not a question of liberating a territory in order to hold elections there that would only be recognized as valid by their organizers, as is the custom. On that subject, you have the poor example of the Paris Commune.

Even if elections could be seriously be organized in this kind of situation, it would only dissociate decision from action and resurrect the political professional. Elections presume that voters be registered and mapped.

The setting up of an administration on the basis of elections presupposes the existence of this administration! It's not power and the state that are born of elections, but the reverse.

Mass revolutionary organizations will be formed and reinforced in accordance with practical tasks. They'll be born of the actions of a minority. You're never going to see 51% of the population suddenly rushing toward the same goals. This active minority will be distinguished by the fact that they won't organize the rest of the population, but will seek to involve them in the resolution of collective problems. Its success will depend on its ability to compel the participation of far more than 51% of the population.

Communism can't be established by the means of a putsch. Faced against the power of the State and its instruments of repression, communism can only prevail if it can manage to cultivate the more-or-less active participation of a big portion of the population, and to isolate a tiny minority as its adversary.

The proletarian revolution, in breaking the chains of wage labor, will enable and require a mass participation beyond all possible comparison to that of bourgeois political revolutions—even when those revolutions were popular revolutions. Those popular revolutions, which democrats align themselves with, weren't decided democratically. En 1789, if the French had been given the choice, would they have voted for the revolution? In reality, it's because of the archaic nature of the privileges of the nobility that a segment of the population rose up. Driven by the successes and results of their actions, they gradually overcame a worm-riddled system.

The communist party will only rouse an overwhelming majority of the population when it seems like the immediate means of redressing the problems of everyday life. Revolutions don't arise when enough people become revolutionaries. People become revolutionaries when the revolution appears—when they see it as possible and necessary to live differently.

Today, when all the elements of the societal structure support each other, money's disappearance seems impossible. Those who champion it come off as tender dreamers. But in the event that market mechanisms were shut down, continuing to depend on money for your necessities will come off like idiotic acrobatics. People will rally to communism not out of ideology, or even out of disgust for a dying society, but out of simple biological necessity. It'll then become necessary to fend off opportunists, incapable of taking a long-term perspective, who will try to find immediate personal gain in the situation.

Why, if we hold that the revolution has to be borne by the broadest participation possible, don't we pronounce ourselves democrats? It would maybe hinder some of the opposition and win us a few friends. But as it happens, we aren't politicians; a superficial alliance would be more hindrance than help. We need to be clear in order to unite and orient our supporters on solid footing. As to the actual opposition—we don't want to make their jobs easier, but in any case, the things we actually say or want matter little to them. Either they misunderstand or they misrepresent, even at the risk of pilfering a few ideas from the work of revolutionaries in order to spice up their own platform.

Democracy is supposed to be the power of the people, the power of all. The communist revolution doesn't mean to change the form of power, or to give it to the people. It aims to divest it from everyone.

Power always has need of a legitimation external to itself. God for monarchies, the people for democracies, crowned or republican. Is there anything more real about *the people* than there is about God? No; God is a character, an incarnation full of humanity, whereas *the people* tends to be nothing more than a pure abstraction of humanity. This *people* that's invoked to endorse the state is only its own reflection. Between this *people* in notion—this political *people*—and the actual people, diverse, living, stupid or smart, who express themselves in their everyday lives, there's a world of difference.

It's not politics that expresses and incarnates the ideas and the will of human beings; it's human beings who become an apparatus for political opinions. They become abstractions themselves when, voters or militants, they go to profess these opinions.

Why don't communists, who would like to do away with exploitation and wars, renounce the coercions and tactics of dictatorialism?

Do we believe that the dominant classes are going to renounce the use of these means? Do we believe that, during a period of upheaval, the most democratic of states won't cast aside all their fine principles? The most liberal among the propertied, the privileged, and the servants of order will maybe claim to fight for democracy. They won't draw attention to the defense of their actual interests. But there's little chance that they'll fight democratically.

It's in the context of a crisis situation that bourgeois methods should be compared against revolutionary methods. It's hypocritical to oppose the behavior of the most democratic of bourgeois states in peacetime with the behavior of revolutionaries in times of trouble. There's every chance that, in a period of crisis, revolutionaries will prove themselves more humane and more democratic than the champions of law and order.

The strike

Democracy is seeing itself refuted, with the spread of wildcat strikes and uprisings. The outbreak of action doesn't hang on a democratic consultation of the rank and file or their representatives.

A fraction of workers—being the most aggressive, least alienated, and most advantageously situated—are revolting. There's no schism between decision and execution, between those who decide and those who execute.

The fundamental problem isn't necessarily how to rally everybody. From a key position in production, it's possible to force bosses to back down. The work stoppage can be its own goal; it's only a matter of taking a little breather or refusing to do some given job.

It's possible for a walkout by a handful of workers to instigate a general walkout. That's what the world saw happening, on the scale of a nation, during May 1968.

The strike was spreading. It was approved of by a great majority of workers. Rapport was forged in action, and there wouldn't have been some prior consultation with all those who'd find themselves affected.

If the workers had been required to reach a democratic decision on the propriety of opening hostilities, they might have given up. But the example of a small number showed them the way to step into the breach, the fearfulness of management, and the likelihood of success. They were gripped by the atmosphere of struggle and solidarity, better able to overcome the feelings of discouragement and resignation that daily helplessness engenders.

Let's imagine that the strike had been decided by means of a referendum. Things probably would have unfolded in a different way. No more shock of the workers' offensive: the opposition would have been informed of the nature, form, scope, and goals of the movement. Organization would have preceded action and discouraged initiatives. The strikers would have remained more or less passive and, apart from a minority of union members or trade unionists, alienated from their own strike.

When workers begin to radicalize, the democratic moment presents itself more and more as a moment of recuperation. It's a matter of voting on the resumption. Bureaucrats, specialists in negotiation, get back on top.

Democracy becomes the manifestation of giving up. It becomes, visibly, what it already was in essence.

Turning to a sole, sovereign general assembly isn't enough to combat bureaucratization. The assembly can become a privileged venue for manipulation, a mass gathering of segregated and powerless individuals, the apparatus of confused and useless chatter.

General assemblies are necessary. It's necessary to be able to take stock, to assess your strengths, to oversee and to hold accountable delegates and special committees. But the assembly can't manifest as the moment that everything hangs on, for whose benefit the rest of reality is sloughed off.

The party

As the crisis of capital continues to intensify and render visible the vanity of capitalist solutions to this crisis, the communist party will continue reforming itself within the population.

The party's formation isn't the occasion that causes the crisis. It isn't the prerequisite for the assault on capital. Its quantitative and qualitative development, on the contrary, is extremely dependent on the escalation of this crisis. It will aim to guide and facilitate the outcome.

The party isn't a gathering constituted according to some fixed doctrine that would go on expanding without its nature changing. The party isn't something that just exists; it's always being constituted. Bit by bit it emerges, takes on contours and contents that are clearer and clearer. Its nature coheres, and the number of its members increases the more that possibilities take shape for a rupture with the system.

Yet the formation of the party isn't a new and indeterminate phenomenon. The party, such as it arises at some given historical moment, is the resurgence of a movement that eludes these temporal limits. The modern party rekindles its connection with a party whose reality and even memory had been effaced by the counter-revolution.

Outside of insurrectionary times, when communism can only be asserted timidly and haltingly, the party, strictly speaking, is condemned to remain a tiny, overlooked segment of the population. Alongside conscious communists, there are numerous unconscious communists who demonstrate revolutionary exigencies through their behavior. The party, broadly speaking—of those who show themselves to be more or less consciously communist in light of ever-increasing occasions—isn't visible. Its image doesn't take form in the reigning spectacle. Its power, however, makes itself felt on the very level of this spectacle. Publicists and politicians, in order to peddle their wares, make garbled echoings of its hopes. The bourgeois and the bureaucrats tremble before this menace, still nameless and still faceless.

It's contradictory to assert yourself communist in a world that represses communism with whatever it takes. Communists aren't ubermenschen who already live differently than their peers. They aren't immune to the prevailing misery. Their theoretical consciousness carries little weight in transforming their own lives.

It's essential, and in any case inevitable, that conscious communists should appear and that they should take care to understand and prepare for the communist revolution. But you can't compare conscious communists with unconscious communists. What matters is to see how and why communist consciousness develops as a practical necessity.

There are certainly people who call themselves revolutionaries. The production of these "revolutionaries" isn't independent of the escalation of the crisis. The majority among them aren't communists and don't even know what they are or what they want. The desire for revolution presents itself as the last and the most hollow of possible desires in this society. It's an abstraction, cut off from tangible needs and hopes. The "revolutionary" can pontificate on anything, engross himself in questions of strategy, but he's incapable of defining what it is he aspires toward. If he speaks of the transformations to be made, his vision is overhung by the question of power. The society to be built rests on a new distribution of power. What is "wanted" is popular power, student power, power to the councils (+ electrification or automation!), power to the people over their own lives, the power to have power over the power to...

On the contrary, the majority of those who'll be revolutionaries, when the revolution corresponds to tangible needs and possibilities, don't feel the need to call themselves revolutionaries.

It's only in a phase of open confrontation, when there is the possibility of communizing the social body, that the party can cease being only a gathering of common opinions or a product of sporadic action. It can finally become a community of action.

When the proletariat in its entirety participates in the revolution, the party isn't mixed up with the class. It doesn't claim to be nor to represent the proletariat. It is the most lucid and the most determined fraction within it. It coexists, collaborates, or clashes with other fractions more moderate or more subservient to bourgeois apparatuses and ideologies.

Its action can be characterized in one sentence: To create the situation that renders it entirely impossible to go back.

It's normal for oppositions to manifest, between the actions of communists and the behavior of the masses. This isn't a sign of some fundamental antagonism. The party doesn't have to eliminate mass organizations and movements. Councils and other rank-and-file committees don't have to eliminate the party. If either of these two things happened, it would necessarily signify the end, the downfall of the revolution. This antagonistic vision is a legacy of the Russian Revolution and the councilist wave of the twenties. It has only one fault: taking as communist organizations that weren't.

The party will fight for the councils because that struggle can't be dissociated from the struggle for communism—even if on this or that point or organizational mode, communists find themselves in disagreement with the masses.

The party itself, which isn't an organization nor, worse, an institution consolidated from above, will organize itself on the councilist model. It's the meeting of those who set themselves, beyond immediate tasks and concerns, to the defense of the whole of the movement. It needs to designate strongholds to be dismantled, concentrate forces on strategic points, propose solutions.

There's no one organization that will be able to claim that it's the party. The latter never identifies with any one sect or mass organization. The supporters of communism show themselves through what they do, not through membership in some limited grouping. The forms of organization don't need to be fixed or consolidated in advance. They'll be discovered over the course of the movement.

TRACT III

7.

INSURRECTION AND
COMMUNIZATION

The communization of society won't be gradual or peaceful but abrupt and insurrectionary. It won't be some peaceful process that some sufficient number of forces will gradually rally around.

Insurrection and communization are intimately linked. There won't be an insurrection first and then a transformation of social reality, enabled by this insurrection, later. The insurrectionary process draws its strength from communization itself.

There is no intermediary, mixed category of the mode of production between capitalism and communism. The period of transition, or rather the period of rupture, is characterized the contradiction between absolutely communist methods on the one hand and a reality still entirely permeated by mercantilism on the other. It's in this phase that a society of abundance and liberty needs to confront the problems of scarcity and power. It has to eliminate the human and material fallout of an era of slavery, and to neutralize the forces that would remain attached to it.

Violence

The use of violence to achieve their aims—that's what distinguishes revolutionaries from reformists.

The opposition between revolutionaries and reformists isn't so much about strategy and method as it is about the nature of the transformation to be accomplished. Here, obviously, arises a difference in method.

History has distinguished two kinds of reformists: the soft and the tough.

Soft reformists, social democrats and parliamentarists,[1] think that their alterations can be made with a soft touch. They're often right, so long as their illusions center on the depth of the reforms that they're capable of actually implementing. They prove every day, and in every corner of the world, that the forces in power are fine with not repressing those who don't threaten them. Sometimes these soft reformists grow tough, but that toughness is wielded chiefly against the proletariat.

Besides these, there are the real toughs, which is to say Stalinists and the like. These take themselves for revolutionaries. Their goal is to seize the state and control the economy by replacing the leaders in power. It isn't worth their while to underestimate their adversaries' ability to retaliate. Their success, and their very skins, depend on it.

And the revolutionaries?

The communist revolution is a tremendous social convulsion. It entails confrontation and violence. But if the revolution is an act of force, its essential question isn't a question of violence, and the terms for its success aren't intrinsically a matter of military force.

This is because the revolution isn't a matter of power. We aren't contesting the state or the economy with all the powerful still in place. Thanks to the positions that it occupies in the economy, communism will be more than capable of disarming the counterrevolution and undermining its foundations, especially in the military. It'll avoid direct confrontation as far as possible.

The reason communist revolution doesn't make violence the central problem is that its aim is to bring about the dawning of what already exists,

---

1   Calque of *parliamentarianiste* (noun): partisan of democratic parliamentarianism.

not to shoehorn some project into reality.

Just as we're opposed to fanatics and fetishists, we're also opposed to pacifists. As much as nonviolent methods can and must be adopted, even with regard to soldiers, nonviolent ideologies can't be tolerated.

This ideology relies on and conveys pedagogical illusions. It assumes that all people can be coached into nonviolence and mobilized with cool heads. It seeks mass action but doesn't see that the problems of information and coordination imposed by this type of action—and retaliation—can't be resolved without the possibility of violence.

Systematic non-violence presumes a consensus between adversaries to respect certain rules and, above all, some freedom of information. Nonviolence is primarily effective as a defensive strategy. Its limitations reveal themselves when it comes to taking the initiative and neutralizing enemies.

The more that the revolution makes itself felt with force and lucidity, the more that it enforces its choices and presents them as irreversible, the more capable it'll be of rallying the hesitant and neutralizing the opposition. An understanding of violence's limited but essential role can avert mistakes with bloody consequences.

The proletariat can't renounce the acquisition, production, and use of weapons. If weapons aren't always readily available in society, the materials that enable their manufacture often are, and in large quantities. It's essential to inventory them and to prepare for their possible use—to arm ourselves and prepare traps that'll force our enemies to pay dearly for their intrusions. What's actually ridiculous and shameful is to push people to form self-defense groups, to equip themselves with revolvers or knives, for defending their factories and neighborhoods against tanks and aircraft.

We can't predict the way that future insurrections will unfold, but we can champion a strategy in advance, over the course of the movement. This strategy is founded on the very nature of the communist revolution and on each person's strengths.

The bourgeois and the bureaucrats are counting on the army. The strength of the proletariat is in its economic position.

The armed forces are vulnerable, but not so much from a military perspective as from its dependency on the economy, More and more, it depends on the economy for its weapons, its munitions, its food, its transportation. It integrates workers and technicians into its core. To wage war—and modern war is costly—logistics has to keep up and the country has to work.

The military counterrevolution must be attacked behind its economic lines. Social peace cannot be allowed to persist at home; it's crucial to denying national armies the ability to mete out repression overseas.

Members of the military know the risk there would be for them to have to compensate for the "failings" of workers in the realm of production. The military can't organize the economy against workers. It prefers to have well-defined adversaries of the same nature as itself over having to accomplish tasks that are alien to it—tasks that bog them down and ultimately dispel them.

The military

It's typical to picture the revolution as a clash between two armies: one under the orders of the privileged and the exploiters, the other at the service of the proletarians. The revolution is reduced to a war. The stakes become the taking of power and the controlling of territories. This vision is dangerously incorrect. It relies on memories of the battles of the Russian and Spanish Civil Wars, as well as of wars for national liberation.

Even if, at some given moment, in some given circumstance, revolutionary action takes a military turn—commando operations, air raids—that'll change nothing about the profound nature and the global character of the conflict.

Not only is it not communist to see the revolution as a confrontation between Red and White armies, it's also moronic, given the disproportion of the military forces involved. To offer capital a war would be to play right into its hands.

The army and the police constitute the last bastion of capital. Their actions can be expressed directly through the destruction of men and of things, but also in creating and maintaining a situation of scarcity suitable for fostering selfishness, fear, and other old instincts. This would pit needy populations against revolutionary troublemakers and tend to reanimate market mechanisms.

The military can be utilized to operate and control certain strategic sectors of the economy.

Because of its hierarchized nature that eliminates discussion and dissent in favor of obedience and discipline—because of its function and its patriotic ideology—the military tends to be a conservative body.

But the military counterrevolution has its weaknesses.

The feeling of security and the sense of great entitlement, which members of the military derive from their enclaves and their trinkets, are in constant danger of being quickly upset if the military can't justify and fortify itself through confrontations with hostile armies on well-defined battlefields. The military must be prevented from functioning as a military, opposed with the dissolving fluidity of communism. It's all about paralyzing, contaminating, dividing, and dispersing military forces.

Our armed interventions need to closely accompany our actions toward social deconstruction and reconstruction. The use of violence can't become an autonomous activity that justifies itself. It serves to block and unblock those situations that depend directly on communization, which provides not only its justification but also its strength.

Before and during an insurrectionary period, you can never be too careful about isolated violence, about terrorism. Revolutionaries can find themselves caught in a cycle of conflict and retaliation that ends up being void of communism. When violence becomes a violence *for* communism and no longer *accompanying* communism—when it's emptied of its immediate content—all provocations become fair game. It becomes easy to perpetrate killings and bombings and pin them on revolutionaries.

Soldiers have to have the rug pulled out from beneath them, deprived of anything to defend, via the immediate and radical transformation of social organization. The military is a tool; it can't do everything by itself, in its capacity as an organ of violence. You can do anything with a bayonet except sit on it.

Among the left, there's a prejudice favoring intellectuals and disfavoring soldiers. When it comes to the revolution, people naturally think that the former will side with it and the latter against it. Intelligence on one side, brute force on the other.

History's shown the extent of the error that these prejudices encompass. Ever since the Paris Commune, when Colonel Rossel sided with the insurgents and was shot for it, and when the progressivist writers G. Sand and E. Zola turned their noses up at those same insurgents,[2] some portion of the armed forces has regularly joined the insurrection and some no-less-notable portion of the intelligentsia has stood against it.

The revolution is such that, when it comes, it will at times frighten those who hoped for it and delight those who dreaded it.

The army forms a fairly autonomous body whose values are alien, in part, to values that are strictly bourgeois and commercial. The bourgeois class, unlike the feudal class, is unable to take direct charge of its own defense. It delegates that to the military or the police. Even if some portion of the military leadership completely identifies its interests with those of the dominant class, there nevertheless exists a latent contradiction between the

---

2   George Sand (1804-76) and Émile Zola (1840-1902). Sand was among the harshest of the Commune's critics, decrying its violence and justifying its brutal repression.

interests and behavior of soldiers and those of the bourgeoisie.

It shouldn't be hoped that the military, or some part of the military, will spontaneously and readily align itself with the revolution. That can only happen as a very function of the revolution's development and infiltration into the military. The military will become revolutionary to the extent that, under pressure from soldiers and officers, the hierarchy's omnipotence is called into question and blind obedience condemned.

Revolutionaries must not make any concession to militarism. Soldiers need to be shown that they're not fighting on their own behalf, and even less on behalf of the Nation. They need to be shown that the movement of capital undermines their ideals. They also need to be shown that, as men, and as men with their distinct abilities and qualities, soldiers do have their place in the communist movement.

Our goal is the destruction of the military. It has to be hoped that this can be realized with the fewest possible confrontations with soldiers. Armed groups, newly constituted or reconstituted, will gradually lose their specific character by participating in productive tasks and workers' councils.

The revolution cannot disregard its strength and lose the opportunity, in transforming the old society's organs of repression, to integrate them into its forces. The cop might be entirely willing to serve what he sees no longer as subversion but as the new authority. It can even be hoped that some won't want to be henchmen any more.

In any case, revolutionaries and proletarians can't allow others to hold a monopoly on armament. This question, of the armament of the proletariat, will be a test to assess the value of rallying soldiers to the revolution.

Vengeance

Revolutionaries have neither a taste for blood nor a spirit of vengeance. The insurrections of the past show that only a small part of the blood spilled, generally, is attributable to insurgents. Hope purges resentment.

It's the counterrevolution that has massacred, imprisoned, deported. Blood flows during battles but often afterward as well, when military victory is already assured—murderous fury, born of the terror of the propertied. The reaction must crush the opposing forces. To the reaction, the revolution seems to reside within the revolutionaries. It must therefore destroy them.

The spirit of vengeance may have played a role in workers' uprisings. But what's that, when you compare their actions to the repression of the Versaillais, of the Kuomingtang in 1927, of the Francoists?

Workers' uprisings have been far less vengeful than the anti-feudal peasants' revolts were. This is because revolution isn't an act of desperation. Destruction of goods, reprisals against individuals—these are often the work of people who see no way out of poverty, contenting themselves with annihilating that which embodies oppression.

Taking revenge wouldn't only be petty, it'd be stupid. To condemn in advance, on the basis of the past, is to fortify our adversaries with fear and determination. It can only create enemies in our midst who, right or wrong, think that they have something to hide. It encourages personal score-settling.

We have to offer our adversaries the opportunity to switch camps. Communist principles don't dictate, in themselves, a uniform mode of conduct. To the contrary, they imply that it's possible to express all the diversity of the characters, situations, and backgrounds of those who participate in the revolution. Better, they imply that if our adversaries can blind themselves so as to no longer see us as anything but "red rats," we must, for our own part, continue to recognize human beings in even the worst of our enemies—without deluding ourselves, incidentally, about human nature.

It'd be stupid to alienate doctors, engineers, and peasants, when many of them will be ready to join us without our having to make any concessions to the myth of the specialist, to the hierarchy of labor, to property. This means that councils will sometimes have to protect certain established positions.

This will go against equality, but it'll make it possible to win certain people over by allowing them to hold onto the things that they value. Doctors can be guaranteed the use of their homes and their professional equipment, on the condition that they don't emigrate and that they treat those who need it. Secondary residences located in the countryside can revert to their legitimate owners—or to relations or friends—without anyone being allowed to have two homes while others live in shacks.

Those who seek to preserve their privileges, on the other hand, or to line their pockets by taking advantage of the situation, will have to understand that they won't enjoy any mercy from their victims.

The more assertive the revolutionary councils are, the more they'll be able to prescribe clear rules, the more they'll be able to promptly transform reality, the less that violence will be necessary.

Redevelopment

Communizing doesn't mean expelling bosses from businesses and factories in order to cling to these institutions; it means starting out by closing a good number of them.

The border between the counterrevolution and the revolution will be drawn between those who push worker-consumers to cling to their yokes and their drugs—in the name of the fatherland, of democracy, of self-management, of workers' councils, of Christ the King, of chocolate pudding, of whatever—and those who push to massively reduce and radically redevelop all production. This will be a matter of reducing pollution, and of breaking with the stupefaction of work and the pseudo-abundance of the market, as quickly as possible,

To remain in your factory, even for the purpose of self-managing it, is to freeze the situation to the benefit of the counterrevolution. Whether professed by workaholics, naive trade unionists, or capitalist scoundrels hoping to buy time, the result of this attitude is all the same.

Revolutionaries will probably find themselves accused, by all these good apostles, of wanting to disrupt production and lower the living standards of the people.

This reduction in production shouldn't at all be seen as some fascination with austerity. The sacrifices demanded will be far fewer than those that would be imposed by any other solution—false solutions that would only serve to prevent a decisive rupture from the past, and to immobilize the forces necessary to the struggle. False solutions that would unite all those who fear seeing the foundations of their power evaporate: die-hard trade unionists, top management and middle managers, politicians, administrators, bosses...

Only by breaking down the division between enterprises and stopping the production of a myriad of products that are barely useful, useless, or even harmful, will it be possible to concentrate forces in order to produce an abundance of things that are needful and necessary. Research has to be undertaken and implementation initiated toward a new system of production. In this way, communization not only signifies demonetization but also the rapid transformation of production. The two things are intimately linked.

Workers, employees, and teachers will be invited to go where they'll be truly useful. These changes will be based primarily on the masses' spontaneous disgust for their work and the revelation they'll have of their own abilities. These changes won't take place under the aegis of a central authority, but will emerge from a multitude of diverse initiatives. This doesn't mean disorder and sloppiness. All revolution entails a degree of fluctuation, of disorder and waste; it's important to keep that to a minimum. This is the particular job of the most radical people. We're neither against order nor against discipline, nor against organization, nor even against authority. Those who would confound revolution with chaos need to be denounced and combated as resolutely as we'll go after the statists whose hands they play into.

Redevelopment must first make it possible to ensure the satisfaction of the most basic needs. Then it must promote not than the creation of certain products but the creation of tools and machinery necessary to their fabrication. These materials will be widely distributed amongst the population, allowing each person to manufacture what they would otherwise have to have manufactured by others.

The following are some signs of the conceivable changes, depending on major economic sectors. None of these transformations make sense in themselves. The danger of making concrete proposals is that they can be co-opted against communism. But it shouldn't be forgotten that revolutionaries can't content themselves with pronouncing general principles—that they must advance concrete solutions in accordance with given circumstances.

Energy: There will be a significant reduction in energy production. This reduction will flow naturally from shuttering the portion of industry that consumes the majority of this energy. It may be necessitated, in any case, by the difficulty of ensuring the supply of oil, gas, coal.

The distribution of energy will be transformed. Some portion that had previously been monopolized by industry will be possible to redirect toward domestic consumption: heating, lighting, the powering of small machines.

New sources of energy will gradually be put in play. It'll be necessary to develop those that pollute the least, and to conserve limited resources like fossil fuels. It'll be possible to promote a decentralized and intermittent form of production for local use. This doesn't mean, in any case, that communism would be fundamentally opposed to nuclear energy. There will simply need to be serious guarantees on production conditions and usage requirements. In the short term, water, wind, and solar seem preferable.

Transportation: Transportation wastes energy, creates pollution, reifies social inequalities... Here, again, there are going to be significant reductions and rationalizations that will enable a reorganization of space. People will manage things in order to avoid making excessively long journeys. They'll have fewer occasions to travel against their wishes. Schedules that are more flexible will allow them to avoid being crammed into the same vehicles at the same time.

The production of present-day automobiles can generally be stopped. The number of cars currently in circulation, used in a more rational way, will make it possible to await the development and manufacture of less miserable machines. Some vehicles can be used as taxis, with or without a driver, or for public purposes.

The vast majority of cars will probably continue to be used privately. This will make it possible to preserve traditional habits and keep users interested in the good working order of what has continued to belong to them. This ownership could be limited by certain conditions of use, aimed at restricting or eliminating traffic in certain places, and at allowing for the best usage and utilization possible.

Trains and other modes of guided transit will have to be promoted and developed. Here, again, is where you can find the greatest safety, the greatest energy efficiency, the most efficient use of land. These fast and comfortable machines can be supplemented by slower vehicles, more individual and more flexible, equipped with non-polluting engines.

In the meantime, production can continue on trucks, bicycles, scooters, and good shoes.

To reduce the need for travel, particularly as concerns rapid connections over long distances, it'll be necessary to develop a good telephone or video-phone network. This will allow for many more people to stay in contact, and at much lower cost, than today.

Airplanes are a noisy, polluting gimmick for businessmen and harried tourists. It'd be difficult to extend their use to everyone. They'll therefore need to be eliminated or limited to certain specific cases.

For long-distance travel, why not modernize big sailboats and bring them back into fashion? Their manufacture would give rise to healthy competition. In any case, there are going to be other ways of getting from one continent to another. For that, there's no need for supersonic aircraft.

Publishing: This is a sector whose revolutionary significance is easy to see. Who's going to control the press?

In insurrectionary periods, workers have regularly controlled the contents of the newspapers they print. With all due respect to those champions of the freedom of the press—who are often no more than supporters of the freedom of the dough—this will begin again. But it isn't enough. The press will have to be transformed. It has to cease being a contemplative reflection of reality.

The revolution will allow for a freedom of expression that's impossible today. A great number of small printing presses, which today belong to businesses and administrations, will be made available to all.

Tomorrow, books and writings won't be edited and distributed depending on the consent of some editor. They'll be taken direct charge of and printed, to start with, by those concerned. Their success will therefore depend on their authors' fortitude and the practical support they meet with.

Today, a considerable portion of a book's cost hangs on its distribution and advertising. Communism's advantage is evident there. It might even become admissible, so as to save the trees, that newspapers and texts be posted up or passed from hand to hand.

Communism, while promoting written, oral, and audiovisual expression for all, must make it possible to reduce society's consumption of paper and ink.

What's to become of literature? No doubt that it'll be transformed, and that the novelistic activity will gradually lose its necessity. Even if people continue to busy themselves with fiction, there will no longer be a world of books in opposition to the real world. Maybe, over time, written communication will even lose its importance and begin to disappear.

Construction: The construction industry will undergo a transformation. This doesn't mean that masons will be put out of work. Construction is one of the rare activities that won't wane.

It'll nevertheless be necessary to take measures to limit or, more radically, ban construction in overcrowded cities and suburbs. But the people who move out of these urban centers are going to need housing. It'll be necessary to begin construction on houses and buildings of every kind. It'll also be necessary to do demolitions and organize the recycling of materials.

Here as elsewhere, and maybe even more quickly, professionalization will be eroded. Those who want a new home are going to have to get their hands dirty. They can seek help from those who know better than them, by training or by experience.

The inadequately housed will be immediately rehoused in apartments and residences that have become vacant for one reason or another. Naturally, one of the first manifestations of the revolution will be a moratorium on the payment of rent and bills.

Clothing: It won't be possible to transform everything all in one go. It'll be necessary to continue producing in accordance with existing materials and machinery—but transformations can certainly be brought about fairly quickly, in terms of quality and durability.

Some number of styles in clothing and shoes will be possible to produce in large quantities. In complement, the production of fabrics and small machines will be cultivated so that people can fashion what they need for themselves. This will allow for products that are adapted to people's tastes. This will allow the distribution of clothing to depend directly on efforts furnished.

Food: The industrialization of food products has generally resulted in a deterioration in quality of said products. Communism must, as quickly as possible, increase the quantity of food produced; alter its distribution, particularly in aid of the Third World's underfed populations; and work toward improvements in quality.

Modifications will be introduced in the composition of products. Anything that's harmful or merely useless, anything that only serves to deceive the consumer, will have to be gotten rid of. Packaging will be simplified.

As far as agriculture's concerned, the use of chemical products has to be limited and gradually reduced. This isn't about some principled position against anything that might be chemical or artificial, but rather an opposition to the real deterioration and adulteration of agricultural products.

Monoculture will have to give way to polyculture and the union of agriculture and livestock farming, which allows for the recycling and utilization of manure and waste. This makes it possible to reduce the scale of outside supplies—which is of vital importance, particularly for non-industrialized countries.

It's more worthwhile for society's forces to be directly invested in working the land, rather than in factories for chemical products and fertilizers. Even if it means diverting hands from agriculture, it'd still be for the best to manufacture agricultural tools and machinery. This equipment needs to be introduced, in particular, to the agricultures of the Third World.

Research on food quality and agricultural methods, which currently is relatively little-developed, needs to be expanded. It'll be necessary to determine the best plant varietals, the methods least taxing on the soil, the crop distribution best adapted to alimentary needs. In agriculture, as elsewhere, there are choices to be made: should we promote animal or vegetable proteins? Should we favor yield or hardiness?

Health: Health problems are, in large part, caused by living and working conditions. In revolutionizing these conditions, communism is going to do much for the health of the population.

Emphasis needs to be placed on measures of sanitation and prevention. The production of drugs will thereby be reduced. Some products that are useless, or that currently only appear useful, will be pulled. Just as with brands of detergent, there exist numerous commodities for the same phar-maceutical product. The costs of packaging, of advertising, outstrip the costs of the actual active ingredients. All of this will obviously disappear.

It's all about deprofessionalizing medicine as rapidly as possible. This means reintroducing medical and sanitary knowledge that's been lost to the population, making it possible to employ medicinal plants. This means training a segment of the population to be able to make medical interven-tions, and within a relatively short amount of time.

Education: The period of insurrection and redevelopment will increase the need for education and training. Since a large portion of the population will have to change occupations, and since everyone will have to diversify their skills, learning will become a necessity.

This learning will be done, in large part, on the job. Everyone will have to share their knowledge to the benefit of their peers.

Television and radio will make it possible to transmit what people need at minimal cost. It'll be easy to broadcast courses in mechanics, in agricul-ture, in masonry, which will supplement practical training.

What's to become of teachers? It's not a question of banning them from teaching—but they will have to be discouraged, by all means, from being teachers and nothing else. In any case, a great part of culture will no longer be made the object of instruction, in the strict sense. As far as children are concerned, it won't be a matter of forcibly removing them from the care of teachers who love their profession. But from the moment that the activities offered to children diversify and expand, from the moment that they're no longer a burden on adults who are themselves no longer chained to profes-sional and domestic labor, it'll become impossible for the school to keep up.

To ensure their own well-being, the teaching profession will have every interest in dedicating themselves to practical tasks, just like everyone else. If they don't, it's them who'll pay the direct costs. No doubt that the major-ity of teachers, who are more and more becoming teaching machines, will appreciate a new way of life—one that wouldn't prevent them, in any case, from benefiting others with their knowledge.

Religion: Some believers of little faith cry that the communist revolution will get rid of religion. This is doubting the Lord's power to see to his own affairs. As for us, we leave the task to him.

Rupture

Between capitalism and communism, there exists a phase not of transition but of rupture, wherein revolutionaries must seek to implement irreversible measures.

Some people lament the commodification and industrialization of all social life. They'd very much like for this to change, but they'd prefer to stay reasonable. They appeal to the authorities in power, or to their official opposition, to promote change. Above all, they'd like for things to change in an orderly way. For them, the irruption of the masses onto the stage of history can only lead to the most inextricable disorder.

They'd like to progressively decommodify the economy by cultivating public services and free goods. Wage labor would be reduced, and alongside it would be developed new activities that are less inhumane.

The most audacious foresee the eventual disappearance of wage labor and the commodity.

It's always the same hope of being able to muzzle and harness capital. The same illusion is propagated by people who want to preserve wage labor while eliminating differences in wage, or while transforming wages into a fair compensation for the onerousness of the work.

Capital is fundamentally expansionist and imperialist. That's why it tends to take over all social life. Non-market sectors, operating alongside a market system, are quickly recommodified. Either they remain pastimes or games completely dependent on capital, like present-day home improve-ment, or they assume greater significance and their production spreads, and so they reinvent capitalism for themselves. There's disintegration from within and an onslaught from without. "Free" producers, those weekend artisans who continue being prisoners of a bourgeois way of life, very nat-urally seek to draw income from their unofficial production so as to earn a little extra cash.

Should we count on political power to support such a "revolution"? This would be forgetting its dependence on the economy. It would be opposing market totalitarianism with state totalitarianism.

Can we count on a transformation of the mind? This would be believing that commodification is primarily a perversion of the intellect. Minds will be what circumstances allow them to be.

You can't reach for the new world with one hand while guarding your wallet with the other.

These reformist notions understand nothing of the necessity of a global rupture, nor the nature of revolutionary proletarian action. They don't see that it's in the circumstances and actions of the dispossessed class that the true adversary of the commodity system will be found. They believe it's possible to take measures against capital because they consider it as a thing whose power must be limited, not as a social relation.

Capital can play around at liberating human activity and decommodi-fying it in appearance. It sells a new life in its all-inclusive resorts; people pay so as to not have to pay. New systems of payment are tending to avoid direct and oppressive contact with money. All of this demonstrates the need for and the possibilities of communism, but also the co-opting, vampiric, deceitful nature of capital.

The commodity system is a whole. It will be cast down in whole. You can't communize sectors one at a time, sectors that are intimately linked by exchange. In any case, does anyone believe that it's possible to limit the field of the intervention in an insurrection?

Fittingly, "anti-market" measures, which aim to temporarily restrict or obscure the actions of capital, can only intend to deter or halt an insurrection. Whatever the goodwill or even the half-understanding of those who propose them, they can only serve the counterrevolution.

In an insurrectionary period, revolutionaries will have to do their best to denounce falsely radical measures and accelerate the course of things. Very often, their actions will be underhandedly denounced, not as revolutionary but as excessive, by those who disguise themselves as revolutionaries in order to better combat the revolution.

The solution to the significant problems posed by the abrupt rupture with the commodity economy will rest, before all else, on the councilist organization of the production and distribution of goods. In this intermediary phase, distinctions due to product scarcity will no longer be made on the basis of money, but by councils and committees of "consumers," who will see to the distribution of products in accordance with their best possible use. The danger is in believing that it's possible to establish a mixed system in order to avoid difficulties.

Councils will have to settle difficult questions, but they're the only force capable of settling them.

To enable and support councilist organization, the working wing of the revolution will need to concentrate its forces on certain strategic points. It'll have to destroy everything that would allow for the survival or resurgence of the old system.

The banking and financial system will have to be destroyed in its material foundations. It'll be necessary to attack establishments, to burn account books, papers, archives. Everything that might resemble a means of payment will have to be eradicated.

The machine of state will have to be paralyzed. This doesn't mean delivering a frontal assault to the center of the system, so much as destroying its manifold tentacles. The state has branches everywhere. This is its strength and its weakness.

Everything that makes it possible to surveil people will have to be tackled, starting with identity papers of every kind. Records, state and private, will have to be hunted down. Apart from a few items of revolutionary or historical interest, administrative archives and papers of all kinds will have to be destroyed.

The seizure of the prisons and the liberation of the prisoners, including political prisoners, will be the order of the day. There's something that won't reassure any upstanding citizens: the entire underworld out on the streets, overnight. *Aren't prisons filled with awful gangsters and horrible killers?*

In reality, most prisoners are proletarians who sought, in attacking property and the commodity, to escape their circumstances. They aren't little saints or benevolent revolutionaries, for the most part. But the reasons for their offenses would vanish with the disappearance of the current system. The overwhelming majority of them will know to put their talents to use at the service to the revolution.

And the underworld? Crooks aren't generally behind bars. Sometimes, they even strike with the collusion of the police. Killers? They often have the law on their side. Some can even be found at the heads of states.

The liberation of prisoners will exclude notorious reprobates and counterrevolutionaries. The end of the commodity, the organization of armed militias, will make it possible to reduce the number of bad actors.

These varying measures can't be carried out within just any context or any balance of power. But they're a pressing necessity for revolutionaries and anti-statists.

Committees entailing the distribution of goods might seek to rally small business owners and managers and use their premises. If these social categories demonstrate an ability to be retrained, all the better. If they resist and seek to retain ownership of their stock and their stores, society will have to do without them. In the case that the commodities that they hold are significant or necessary, they'll have to be seized. In any case, their power is limited, as it'll suffice to cut off their supplies at the source.

Advertising can be redeveloped as anti-advertising. This will be a matter of providing information on the characteristics and the manufacture of products, on the status of reserves, and encouraging moderation.

Internationalism

The revolution will be global.

This isn't a moral imperative—*all men are equal, and brothers, and have a right to it.*

The revolution will be global because capital itself is a global reality. It's destroyed human communities, separated individuals, made every person into the competitor of every other. But by the same stroke, it's collected and unified the human race under its heel. Today, and for the first time in history since Adam and Eve, there's a correspondence between the genetic unity and the social unity of the species.

The birth of the national idea and the nation-state are the direct fruit of capitalist development, of the destruction of traditional groups, of standardization through trade, of inequality in growth. But if capital takes shelter behind borders, it doesn't let them imprison it. Its development, imperialistic and commonplace, has always had the tendency to conquer and unify markets. There has been a succession of different countries and regions that were the preferred site of capital accumulation, before declining so as to make way for the next.

The contemporary era has seen this movement accelerate. There's been a globalization of commodity relations and an escalation in inequality. Colonization, world wars, the development of new poles of accumulation, the formation of new nation-states, more or less puppets—these have been the stages of the movement. The proliferation of nations and states hasn't prevented the consolidation, even on the political level. Small states are enfeoffed to stronger states; they come together into military blocs and economic zones; they create global institutions and peace-keeping forces.

Even more remarkable is the internationalization of trade and the formation of multinational businesses, which have outpaced political consolidation and deprived states of the greater part of their economic power. These giant firms are richer than many nations. They have a planetary view of things. They seek to produce and to sell wherever it's most profitable, with no regard for borders.

Trade is standardizing life across the world; the same kinds of grains, buildings, and teachings can be found throughout. Local color, preserved or superimposed, is an advertising pitch aimed at tourists and traditionalists. Nothing better illustrates this gimmickification of the national idea than the archetypal scenery transported around the world on interchangeable airplanes. Here you eat à la française, there you run into some Japanese geishas... and just about everywhere, Palestinian hijackers.

Faced with all of this, revolutionaries obviously aren't calling for the defense or the restoration of the homeland, as are a heap of demagogues. Nor do we support regionalist or neo-nationalist movements that advocate the formation of newer, more legitimate homelands. In invoking the right to difference and autonomy, what's being opposed is nationalism with nationalism, state with state. At first, there's often a healthy reaction against statism, standardization, and the inequality of development in the contemporary world. The only solution possible is the end of capital and all of its states.

Communism isn't the enemy of homelands, if by *love of the homeland* you mean the attachment of men to their regions, landscapes, customs, local ways of life. We don't want to revive parochial attitudes, but we're against the leveling of countries and their inhabitants.

Pretty often, defenders of the homeland are nothing more than defenders of the state. Their nostalgia seeks to ignore what it is that's destroying the values that they defend.

Nationalism developed, paradoxically, in lockstep with the deterioration of man's attachment to and knowledge of his environment. It valorizes not a real community but the image of a community that expresses the moronic fetishism of the flag or of national heroes. More and more, our era is rendering all of this bric-a-brac obsolete. The feelings that they crystallize around are more and more hypocritical and detached from reality.

Most leaders who glorify the national idea cancel each other out. Time and again, the ruling and privileged classes have shown how little they regard patriotism. The nation's interests are only as worthwhile as their correspondence with the interests of capital. In the event that some proletarian menace were to appear, the ruling classes of various countries would rush to make peace.

The revolution will be global because the problems it will have to solve are global. The interpenetration of different economies prevents any solitary escape. In any case, if the revolution develops in a single country, it'll have to face off against the outside counterrevolution. But this interdependence, the development of the means of communication, the simultaneity of economic and political upheavals, will make the revolution more infectious than ever. Each state, in playing policeman elsewhere, will have worry about accelerating things at home. The more quickly the insurrection spreads, the more difficult its repression will become.

Hunger and pollution have no local causes, even if their effects are very localized. The revolution will have to establish universal rules for the protection of nature. Agriculture will have to be organized so as to meet the needs of all populations.

This isn't to say that rich, industrialized countries will have to bleed themselves dry, or that poor countries will remain dependent on privileged regions.

Each region, in accordance with its problems and its resources, with the stature of its proletariat, will have to come up with its specific forms of organization and development. As much as possible, they'll have to manage with local resources to begin with.

It'll nevertheless be necessary to organize transfers of equipment and technicians, especially at the start, in order to help the most marginalized escape abject poverty as quickly as possible. Food consumption in some regions will have to be reduced or transformed, if necessary, to help others. Communists will always be at the vanguard of the fight against local self-interest.

Underdeveloped countries can be communized, despite the deficiency of their development. The possibility of communism is established on a global scale. What matters isn't the quantitative development so much as the qualitative development of productive forces. A certain degree of science and technology will generate a quantitative abundance in short time. The current predominance of industrialized countries will serve the dawn of communism by supporting local proletarian forces to liquidate capital everywhere.

How do you promote communist transformations in countries where agrarian populations predominate? There will be no need to have another go at primitive accumulation. Unlike capitalism, communism won't establish itself by wreaking havoc on traditional social structures. On the contrary, by ridding them of their most negative aspects, communism will be able to build itself upon these structures to rediscover, beneath the parasitism and feudalism, their essential peasant communities.

This won't prevent an attendant development of modern activities. Within these communities, technologies can be introduced: lightweight agricultural equipment, energy sensors, contraceptive procedures, medical treatments... There's no absolute incompatibility between the equilibrium of the traditional community and the implementation of easy-to-use technologies. There are already examples of primitive populations who know how to use modern technologies. The actual handicap is rather the disintegration of these communities under the influence of capital.

It's practically certain that the populations and social structures in question will evolve. But this evolution won't primarily have been a destruction of men and a renunciation of community values.

Can you count on the working class to establish a global solidarity? Aren't workers often racist?

Workers often show themselves to be racists—racist against foreigners, and foremost against workers who are immigrants or racial minorities. "Working-class" governments have shown themselves to be more racist, particularly on the issue of immigration, than have bourgeois governments. It's often businessmen who are favorable to immigration and the abolition of discriminatory laws.

Working-class racism corresponds firstly to the attitude of the oppressed who, unable to escape their condition, are more than happy to be able to feel superior to their dogs, to cops, to immigrants. It's the expression of a real class interest, of the working class qua commodity. The intellectual can wax poetic about the brotherhood of man; the worker, particularly the unskilled worker, understands very well that the foreigner is first and foremost a competitor in the labor market. Racism, overt or covert, is born of the inability to recognize that it's capital that pits wage laborers against each other. This lack of understanding isn't the manifestation of some straightforward intellectual deficiency. It corresponds to a powerlessness. Understanding goes hand in hand with the ability to transform reality. When the proletariat rises up and comes together, racism crumbles. No need to wait for the revolution to see it; in incomplete struggles, workers of various origins reject prejudices and mistrust.

8.

THE PROLETARIAT
AND COMMUNISM

Communism is the negation of the proletarian condition by the proletarians themselves. The proletariat and communism are realities that are intimately and contradictorily linked. If you separate them, you can understand neither the communist movement, nor the communist revolution, nor even the proletariat.

Lenin

In the wake of Kautsky, Lenin said that proletarians are only capable, by their own might, of rising to a trade-unionist consciousness.[1] They can only dream of selling themselves at greater cost, not of revolutionizing society. Lenin was wrong. Proletarians are incapable of reaching a clear consciousness of their economic interests. Proletarians are merchandise, but they're also paltry merchants. In struggle and negotiation, proletarians consistently

---

1   Following the Bolshevik Revolution, the rift between Lenin and influential German Marxist Karl Kautsky (1854–1938), proponent of gradual socialist change via democracy and parliamentarianism, would deepen into a partisan schism. They had previously agreed, however, on the limitations of trade unionism and its irreconcilability with revolutionary politics and tactics. See "What Is To Be Done?: Burning Questions of Our Movement," in Vladimir Lenin, *Selected Works* (Moscow: Foreign Languages Press, 1946), 1:149–271; and Karl Kautsky, "Trades Unions and Socialism," *The International Socialist Review* 1, no. 10 (April 1901): 593–9.

demonstrate that they don't know what they want and that they muddle and confuse economic and human realities.

This is a weakness, because when it concerns the defense of their economic interests, the proletariat is much less effective than the bourgeoisie. But you can't judge them by a bourgeois standard.

Lenin was right to underscore the discontinuity between trade-unionist consciousness and revolutionary consciousness. The second isn't an intensification of the first. The two are at odds. But revolutionary consciousness—and for us, this is communist consciousness—doesn't have to be imported from outside, isn't the product of intellectuals as a social stratum. Lenin's perspective isn't stupid, as some defenders of the people believe, but it accounts only for an obvious movement. A movement immediately contradicted by a period of revolution.

The proletariat demonstrates daily that it's already beyond the economy. Its ineffectiveness, its naive illusions, are the negative and fleeting inverse of its humanity. In the struggle, independent of the necessarily limited nature of its demands, it manifests its humanity and its aspirations toward communism in many ways and through many slips of the tongue.

What matters isn't what the proletariat is or appears to be when it works, when it parades on May Day, when it responds to opinion polls. Its fundamental situation will compel it, and already does compel it, to act in a communist way.

In order to survive under normal conditions, the proletarian must seek to compensate for this fundamental privation through the thousand means available to him. In the spectacle, he finds himself interests, homelands, drugs. He tries to find a new lease on life through the power of his company or his union. Capital can't abolish widespread prostitution, but it can distract those who prostitute themselves. It lavishes solace on the proletariat by allowing it to "find fulfillment" and become ensnared in commodities and images.

The proletariat isn't the optimistic incarnation of communism within capitalism; neither is it permanently and eternally integrated in a system that sucks it dry of all its sweat and life. Its reality is fundamentally contradictory. All of a sudden, a breach forms. In rushes the proletariat to widen it. The consequences of its actions push it forward. It discovers its strength and does things it never would have dared to dream of.

The bourgeois and the proletarians

What is the proletariat? Where does it start and where does it stop? What's its numerical significance?

On the numerical extent of the working class, strictly speaking, there have been evaluations based on official statistics. It represents only a slight portion of the global population, as its size can be gauged somewhere between 200 and 250 million individuals. This figure excludes the families of these workers and fails to count a good number of proletarianized wage laborers, even in industry, and therefore can't represent all proletarians. In any case, the numerical extent of the working class, which is already enormous when compared to that of the bourgeoisie, is insufficient to account for its true significance.

To add—this significance, contrary to the thesis that avant-garde sociologists are trying to substantiate, is growing.

But just as much as the bourgeoisie, the proletariat isn't something that can be touched, defined, and numbered with precision. This detracts nothing from its reality, even if our sociologists can't manage to snare it in their academic nets.

The proletariat can't be reduced to some standardized image: the indigent in rags, the blue-collar worker, the standard-bearer of the red flag. It's only in specific situations that its limits appear with clarity.

Just as the bourgeois is defined as a caste (by its privileges and its quirks, by the difficulty of entering it) instead of as a class (by its function in the relations of production), so too is the proletariat reduced to a socio-professional category, or to some collection of socio-professional categories.

From there, it's easy to demonstrate that it's difficult, if not impossible, to seize upon just what the proletariat is. *Does it really exist? Haven't technological progress and social security gotten rid of it?* The class struggle, if you consent to grant it any significance, is reduced to one form of conflict among others. Women and men, the young and the old, the cosmopolitan and the countrified all bicker from time to time. Why shouldn't it be the same between workers and bosses?

Our sociologists reproach Marx, he who invented class struggle, of not knowing what a social class is. *He contradicts himself, sometimes speaking of the peasantry as a class and sometimes dividing it into opposing classes.*

That peasants can at times be considered as a single class because they share common interests and illusions, because they act in the same direction—and then that these same peasants can be divided into poor and rich, into farmers and landowners—that's beyond the comprehension of a sociologist. He can't understand that a class isn't defined, from an intellectual point of view as well as from a practical point of view, independently of the activity by which it constitutes a class. There are no classes independent of the class struggle.

Reducing a class to a socio-professional category is to put on the airs of science and rigor. In reality, everything depends on the more-or-less arbitrary criteria with which someone chooses to dissect the social body. More than anything, this objectifies reality.

All is reduced to the place that capital assigns to men. Specific dissections are captured in time: intellectuals, workers, denizens of slums, minimum wage workers. You can see neither what engenders these circumstances nor the possibility of leaving them behind.

At best, "classes" stay classes; one can be imagined to prevail over the other. Thus the bourgeoisie dominates in the West, while the proletariat has installed its dictatorship in Eastern Europe.

For us, the proletariat can't be defined independent of its struggle against capitalism—that is to say, also, independent of communism.

This doesn't mean that a class is a set of people fighting for the same cause. If that were the case, the bourgeois sympathetic to the revolution would transform into proletarians, and the reactionary street sweeper would end up a banker. Anti-capitalism—that is, communism—can become a cause for some, but by nature, it isn't a cause. It's an activity linked to a specific social situation.

The proletariat is that fraction of the population that produces capital while being cut off from its ownership and management. The nightmare of self-management is to make proletarians perform the role of the bourgeoisie. If this pipe dream were to be realized, there still wouldn't be an abolition of classes. The bourgeoisie and the proletariat would coexist, in contradiction, within a single body. One person, operating machinery on the factory floor, would be his own enemy while on the board of directors.

From time to time, it transpires that children of the bourgeoisie go and ruin their health in a factory, or that workers line their pockets at the expense of an unlucky few. There's nothing in this that signifies the abolition of classes.

The line of demarcation between capital's managers and slaves is rigid. It simply happens that some people straddle the border, a foot to either side. They'll very much have to settle on one side or the other.

Should the line of demarcation be made concrete? You can capture it in attitudes toward money. Of course, the bourgeois can be distinguished from the proletarians by the amount of money that passes through their hands—but that's not enough. More fundamentally, the proletarian sees money as money. For him, it represents a certain number of goods. For the bourgeois, money is money capital. Money is for making more money. You invest it and, how wonderful, it's spawned more. This is what links the medieval bourgeois, across the ages, with the modern manager. The hypocrisy continues to this day.

To discern the bourgeois class, it's necessary to also include the familial ties and the sociological burdens that make the children and the wives of the bourgeois members of the bourgeoisie.

In economic life and within businesses, there's a border between those who have access to financial knowledge and decisions—not necessarily the technicians or employees of finance—and the others. There are those who know that a business is money that's been temporarily tied up, meant to make more money, then there's the vast majority: those who see it primarily as the manufacture and trade of use values.

It's sometimes difficult to pin an individual to any particular class. Some senior executive, some engineer, or, why not, some worker, can be caught up by the ruling class by means of his family background, his likelihood of promotion, his friendships, his leadership roles, his possessions, his properties. On the contrary, petty investors are pinned to the dominated class by a thousand ties.

From the perspective of the revolution, it's important to not immediately throw these luxury proletarians into the bourgeois camp. The engineer attached to the bourgeoisie—and all the more so his colleagues who share neither his salary, nor his managerial role, nor his connections—can feel the contradictions between his professional and human interests and the limits imposed by finance. This can push him toward communism, toward a world where technical projects are free of the dictatorship of exchange value.

The knowledge and skills of this group are essential. But beware of those who may be tempted toward the revolution because they see their condition proletarianizing and naively hope to regain authority.

Under normal circumstances, and especially outside of the production process, the situation can seem unclear. Society seems to consist of lone atoms that meander in one direction or another. The worker and the bourgeois seem to disappear, no longer anything more than voters with equal say or consumers with more or less money. But as soon as a conflict erupts, as soon as the revolution appears, these atoms gather around antagonistic poles.

The proletariat isn't an undifferentiated mass. Certain social strata, certain individuals, are a driving force in accordance with their specific attributes and their place in production. To a greater or lesser extent, they help the class to build itself as a class.

Some social strata are more restless, or protest their discontent more loudly, than others. Be wary of appearances. A group that's more disruptive than another might not ultimately prove itself to be very revolutionary. It might be active for reasons that are very specific to it. It might be acting out because its status is waning. But it can't manage to take aim at the foundations of society. With the revolution in sight, it might end up feeling more threatened than capital will.

Those who seem the most integrated and the most quiet, because they're being coddled by the system, might wake up and get straight to the point. The power and the assurance that their situation grants them may empower them to attack capital without compromise.

The evolution of individuals and social strata can't be considered independently of the depth of the conflict and the situation as a whole. Left to their own devices, social strata like students, intellectuals, and executives can only rise to a corporatist consciousness, or worse, a pseudo-revolutionary one. Let communism develop and these strata, by the very virtue of the lack of autonomy that characterizes them, will be radicalized. Not having any real power or interests to defend, they can only find these things by joining and supporting workers.

Can the immense mass of Third World peasants participate in the communist revolution? Is it part of the proletariat? Yes, but not as a function of the degree of its poverty. The more direct capital's hold on its existence, the more it forms a part of the proletariat.

Even if it doesn't labor for wages, it tends to join up with the class of wage laborers, given the commodity economy's growing hold on all men and resources. The offensive of the wage-laboring proletarians will help it to discover its enemy and its solutions.

Wage labor, in a way, is capital's ideal relation of exploitation. Nevertheless, you can't lump together proletarians and wage laborers. It's already been shown that the relations of slavery were integrated into the capitalist world by thus changing their contents. Many small proprietors are directly subject to capitalist exploitation, and often more oppressed by it, than are wage laborers. The leaders of large companies receive wages. In reality, however, everything about them is bourgeois. They set their wages themselves, and this wage is only one part of their real income.

Some professions develop more of a revolutionary attitude than others. The question depends particularly on the degree of identification existing between the worker and his role.

Some get caught up in the game. They can't put things into perspective, regarding the work that they do. Either their work makes them into their own tools and all challenges to their professional roles constitutes a challenge to their own selves, as in the case of educators, or the products of their labors aren't products at all but direct contributions to the functioning of their companies.

In either case, there's a danger of developing a ideology that justifies their professional roles and their contradictions. The most alienated might end up believing that, thanks to their own abilities or to the general usefulness of their toils, they are revolutionizing society.

The most clear-sighted workers are often those who feel no connection to their companies or to the jobs that they occupy. This is the case for most workers.

Given their place in production—the solidarity it engenders, their human qualities—workers will be at the heart of the communist revolution. Even if the American or the Soviet worker has an easier time surviving than the Indian beggar, even if he's more corrupt, he's also better placed to recognize the nature of the oppression that hangs over him and to put an end to it.

It's customary to deny the working class its central role in the revolution.

People highlight its absence from struggles for national liberation, which all the same led to Marxist states.

People pay particular attention to the lack of revolutionary consciousness among the vast majority of workers from rich countries, and to the benefits that they draw from the system.

People entrust other social categories with the role that these workers seem incapable of fulfilling. The revolutions of the 19th century are said to have been the handiwork of artisans. In the 20th century, Leninist intellectuals are said to have taken the reins. In countries of the Third World, it's all about the peasants.

If these people were to look at things soberly, they would see that workers have consistently been at the center of attempts to radically transform reality. Workers are reproached for not having taken part in revolutions that were, in reality, bourgeois. When workers do intervene, people relegate their actions to the backdrop in order to foreground people belonging to social groups that prove themselves to be hardly communist, either up front or after the fact. When proletarians do rise up, people exaggerate and foreground one or another characteristic in order to demonstrate that they're workers only marginally, doubtfully—that they're peasants, petit bourgeois, soldiers, gangsters disguised as workers.

Some modernists replace a gentrified proletariat with new categories. The revolution is said to be the work of young people because they aren't yet domesticated, of women because they're more in touch with the realities of life, of hippies or other nonconformists because they're outside the system, of black people because they love music and have rhythm in their blood... Others no longer see the necessity to give the advantage to any particular category. Capital is an inhuman force to which all are victims; it's therefore humanity, as a species, that needs to rise up. There's no longer a bourgeoisie or a proletariat—or little enough of them, anyway.

When one or another social group, or age group, or sexual category, is foregrounded, it's done by virtue of the values that these groups are said to hold. There isn't so much a change in the choice of revolutionary subject as there is an implicit recognition of reality, such as it is. Young people would be revolutionaries qua young people, women qua women, while the proletariat, which includes both young people and women, is revolutionary only so long as it's no longer the proletariat. The proletariat isn't a social group. It's a movement. It is what it becomes. It exists as a function of its potential for self-destruction.

We aren't saying that young people—or women, or disabled veterans—don't have specific concerns, or that they can't transform reality. Simply put, unless they act as proletarians, they can only defend their concerns as young people—or as women, or as disabled veterans—within some given reality. The proletarian revolution can give them the means, without abandoning their convictions, to go beyond their factional demands, to transcend them. These are young people—women, disabled veterans—who take action, but they no longer do so for youth, for femininity, or for its converse, state benefits and the regard of the citizens.

And the intellectuals?

In a way, the revolution requires that proletarians become intellectuals. They must be capable of going beyond their immediate circumstances. It's well known that during insurrections you see people on the streets, discussing problems that were previously the preserve of philosophers.

The revolution also signifies the end of the intellectual as a separate social category. If intellectuals participate in the revolution, they can only do so by denying their own status—by recognizing that they're crippled. Eventually, measures will need to be taken to prevent anyone from being able to continue on as an intellectual and nothing else.

Intellectuals are often attributed a privileged role as the bearers of consciousness. On its own, consciousness is nothing and can do nothing. Our intellectuals, who've often believed themselves capable of rising to a broad and objective understanding of things, in fact have regularly been in the thrall of the established powers. They've been subject to the worst delusions and have supported, with the spirit of criticality, of course, the worst drivel. Ready to excuse all in the name of Reason, of History, of Progress.

The demands of intellectuals are better suited to stir the hearts of the bourgeois than those of workers. How much nobler it is to demand freedom of expression than to cry out for bread! The intellectual seems to be the champion of the public interest. The worker seems self-centered and earthbound.

Yet proletarian demands are more profound than those of intellectuals. Intellectuals make a specialization of crying out for empty forms. When workers cry out for, or rather impose, freedom of expression, it's because they have something to say. Otherwise, this is of relatively little interest to them. Their ability to avoid dissociating form and content, to avoid fighting over hot air, is a sign of communism. The problem with intellectuals is that hot air is often what they draw their income from.

The youth are often the most active in revolutions. Maybe there are biological causes for this, but their social situation is sufficient explanation. Even those who come from the privileged classes are less tied to the established powers. They have to wait to inherit! Capitalist society fetishizes youth and renewal, but it distances the youth from positions of responsibility and property. They find themselves more available.

In addition to the youth, people sometimes foreground nonconformists. *They don't live like everyone else; maybe they're the future?* Here, again, there's an inability to comprehend that the revolution can and must emerge from within the system itself. There's an inability to understand, dialectically, just what the proletariat is. There's a delusion about the degree of independence that nonconformists enjoy, in relation to the system.

Has capital itself abolished social classes by outpacing the revolution? It's long been claimed that the bourgeois revolution enabled all men to be equal at last.

Society's division into classes is alive and well. Never before has it been so pronounced, perhaps, even if never before have such means been deployed to scrub the fact from memory.

Of course capital's an impersonal force. Of course everyone's more or less subject to its effects. Poor bourgeois, working themselves into the ground, arguing with their children, breathing unwholesome air!

The effects of capital, some have more opportunity to remedy than others. The disparity in today's living conditions is considerably entrenched. The possibilities of diversifying products and the development of trade have made it so that certain strata of the population have a standard and quality of life very alien and superior to that of their contemporaries. It may very well be that the bourgeois aren't the happiest. They can at least quit being bourgeois. The reverse isn't possible for road workers. If even the bourgeois are discontented with their way of life, that's just one more reason for abolishing this class and its society.

The bourgeoisie doesn't posture. It leaves that to new money. It's not in its interest to flaunt the lifestyle it leads in the shelter of its dachas and its private beaches. Proletarians generally overestimate the incomes of the social classes closest to them and underestimate those of the actual bourgeois.

Were the bourgeois to lead an austere and frugal lifestyle, it still wouldn't make them disappear in their capacity as a class. What counts more than anything is their economic and social function. Their income is obviously directly tied to it. A portion of their consumption, including in Western countries, is blended into their business expenses. They travel, they dine, they fuck for and on the company dime.

Now more than ever, capital has the tendency to eat away at the identities of social groups—as much with the bourgeoisie as with the working class. The voter, the consumer, are beyond class. The pleasure kindled by the purchase is no longer tied to status but to impersonal cash. This capitalist negation of the classes makes ready for classless society. But it's negated, in its turn, by the economic necessity that aims to hierarchize incomes and divide roles.

The battle for communism isn't a battle for any particular class, but a struggle for humanity. But this battle is tied to those to whom all humanity is denied. The revolution won't win unanimous support, and it's danger-ous to lead people to believe it will. Maybe a few bourgeois will rally to the movement; that won't change anything about the fact that the interests of the bourgeoisie are at odds with those of communism. The proletarian will immediately gain from the revolution, while the bourgeois will be dis-possessed by it. Though communism applies to the entire human species, there are men who can identify their immediate interests with those of the species, in a period of rupture, and others—not.

Waiting for Godot

What do revolutionaries propose to do, while waiting for the night of the Big Night?[2]

We have no magic bullet for making the time pass, no ideal type of con-duct to champion. Communists, like anyone else, are mired in the muck of capitalism and unable to implement some pure and universal strategy that sees past all specific interests, abilities, and conditions. In any case, we aren't proposing anything for the "masses" that we'd refuse for ourselves, nor vice versa. We can only make note of differences in behavior.

We aren't purists; we accept improvements, however limited, as long as they're real. This is already being thorough at a time when people herald great victories as soon as they've been paid off with hot air.

We aren't purists; we're willing to take action with people who don't share our opinions, in the beginning, from the moment that the prospects for action become clear.

It's worthwhile to be flexible on a practical level in order to take advan-tage of changing circumstances, of the unexpected. It's important to know

---

2   Transliteration of *Grand Soir*, an idiom for revolution.

how to compromise and, above all, how to recognize compromises made. We have no formulas on offer, and we feel sorry for those who need them. No remote guidance here.

Those who act with an obsession for co-opting the revolution are themselves co-opted from the outset, and radically so. Sectarianism is foremost a way to protect yourself from your own doubts. When you have deep convictions—not ideological ones—you can innovate, improvise, and invent without feeling your purity threatened. Mistakes? Well, it's not by smothering the truth against your own breast that you preserve it.

This pragmatic flexibility needs to be accompanied by a serious rigidity and even, let's say, in order to frighten off the "free spirits," doctrinal dogmatism. Theoretical clarity and surety are essential. You have to know where you're going and you have to make it known, too.

Our time is one of rigid behavior and flabby thinking. It's a matter of breaking with that. Ideas are only of interest if they provide sufficiently solid points of reference.

The classic question: *Should you participate in trade unions?* It all depends on the situation, the fellows concerned. *But trade unions have been assimilated?!* That could be a reason to participate in them. Either you take advantage of the benefits this brings the trade unions or you demonstrate the limits of these benefits. Eventually you're run out, and the contradiction between revolutionary content and the trade-unionist form is brought to light.

If participation in trade unions is acceptable, the conquest of their apparatuses in order to retrain them in a revolutionary direction is to be rejected.

In the struggle, as soon as opportunities arise for organization in a broader and less specialized way, trade unions must be rejected. The trade-unionist form can be made useful during a situation of retreat, but it can't be allowed to impede the growth and intensification of the struggle. Actions by and for class must not be opposed with actions by and for an organization of specialists in demands and negotiation. In any case, it's certain that as long as workers remain commodities whose price is up for negotiation, trade union apparatuses will still have a reason to exist.

It isn't by giving up on narrow battles that you prepare yourself for the final fight. It's not by scorning wage issues that you further the abolition of wage labor. Economic irreducibility is a manifestation of the capacity for resistance, and it can become dangerous for the system when threatened at its core—which is to say at its cash register. Woe betide anyone who seeks to distract proletarians from these issues with ideological fumes. Giving up the fight because "the juice isn't worth the squeeze" is often no more than the expression of a more general passivity.

Are we falling into the trap of efficacy for efficacy's sake? Into economism? No, but we believe that class action tends to call forth its own content. It's because of this that powers of all kinds seek to muzzle it.

As advocates for class pressure and class reaction as immediate and varied as possible, we're extremely suspicious of protest goals that are dissociated from immediate possibilities and power relations. Even and especially when it comes to a transitional program of a Trotskyist savor. These representations, which are meant to unify and enlighten the proletariat, only block its view.

As just as it is to fight to reduce the time we spend at work, and in ways that are as generalizable as possible, it's perverse to set targets for the length of the workweek or the age of retirement. All that does is take charge of and internalize capitalist limitations and divisions. The choice is between working time and free time, or, for the elderly, the condition of the convict or that of the dependent. The battle is curbed. Latent communism is sterilized.

Communism is the only defensible prospect. It's not some distant abstraction but the human solution to all problems. It's a matter of making manifest the meaning of the proletarian movement, of showing the power at its disposal.

Often, it's the covert struggles—absenteeism, slowdowns, sabotage, time theft, skimming—that are the most effective. We aren't fetishizing them.

Capital can tolerate them and use them as a safety valve. They can't replace a broader fight. But they bolster a fighting spirit, cultivate initiative, and win some healthy and immediate satisfactions.

It's a question of popularizing those means of action that prefigure the communist world while putting immediate pressure on exploiters. It's often possible, on the sly but also openly and in massive numbers, to distribute products and run services for free. Postal workers could neglect to stamp letters, railway workers to inspect tickets. If the most committed workers are fired, there are always opportunities for sabotage in order to get them reinstated.

Our strategy can be expressed as such: less hot air, less spectacle, but let the working class use the numerous means that it has at its disposal in order to command respect and set the future in motion. A little less solemn dissent and a few more smug and sneering smiles.

On the scale of history, the communist revolution is imminent. We aren't writing for future generations.

While affirming this, we're well aware that numerous revolutionaries have already declared the like and been mistaken. The system's capacity for adaptation has regularly been underestimated. But it seems to us that these days, in reaction, people are doing the opposite. Isn't this capital's last gambit, to have anchored the image of its power and immortality in every head?

Having developed mechanization to the very threshold of automation, having unified the planet, capital is at the height of its power—but it's also reached its historical limits. It can no longer hold up to the destruction of the social fabric or the environmental degradation that it engenders. It can no longer purge its fatty excesses. Its own power, its concentration, is what's turning into a weakness.

The crisis of economic civilization has gradually taken shape as an economic crisis. Poetic justice! But the current phase can't be reduced to a moment of economic difficulties.

To emerge from this crisis, it's necessary to augment the rate of surplus value and straighten out the declining profitability of capital. There are many obstacles, technical, ecological, and human. It can only come about through massive conflicts and upheavals. The proletariat is already showing, in a thousand ways, that it won't let things happen without it. It's also showing that it isn't prepared to adhere to some reformist solution—a solution that could only entail ensuring its complicity in its own defeat and burial, worse than Stalinism or fascism ever did.

9.

A HUMAN
BECOMING

Communism is no prisoner of the future. It arises from within capitalism itself. The activity that proletarians deploy when they spontaneously, and most often unconsciously, reject their condition is communist.

Communism presents itself, first of all, as theory as much as practice; as an anticipation. From the start, it presents itself as a more-or-less feasible—though immediate—solution to the ills of the old world. Utopia isn't some dross to be eliminated. On the contrary, it's the characteristic sign of communism. We have more confidence in the science of the future than in that of the present. But the future does eat away at the present.

Of course communism is a stage of human history, a new world. But more than anything, it's not some given social form; it's a privileged movement in the humanization of the species.

History

On the theoretical plane, communism appeared with the renewal of Renaissance ideas. In Leuven, 1516, Englishman Thomas More published his *Utopia*. In 1602, the Dominican Campanella wrote *The City of the Sun*. He was therefore imprisoned for provoking an anti-Spanish conspiracy in Calabria. This was for having described a world where money, property, and class division disappeared, and for having posed this as an alternative to the world he lived in. More, Campanella, and the others who tended toward communism weren't proletarians, nor even rebels. Rather, they were brilliant, trailblazing minds who either courted the established powers or were hunted down for their independence and nonconformity.

Yet in the same period, with the German Peasants' War and Thomas Müntzer, communism began to materialize. It terrified princes, the bourgeois, and religious reformers like Luther, who cried out, "Lost wretches that you are! It's the voice of flesh and blood that rises in your ears."[1]

They were confusing faith with hope; is it not natural to believe, when one possesses nothing? Now, the grave thing was this: the blessed hope that animated them, they meant to manifest not in another world after death, but on this very earth, and as soon as possible (*The Revolution of the Saints, 1520-1536*, G. d'Aubarède 1946).[2]

But with the Anabaptists of those times, it hadn't only been a question of religion. Their doctrine was undermining the foundations of the entire social order: property, laws, magistrature ... As for private homes, each man made do as he pleased. One such, who had formerly lived beneath a thatched roof, conveyed himself to a hotel. Domestics of the nobility and the clergy helped themselves, without scruple, to what had belonged to their masters. They sacked the episcopal palace, the archives, the titles, the royal grants, all the papers. Of what use could these trifles be, in the new Zion, of which the foundations were doctrinal liberty and fraternal equality? (*Jean Bockelson*, M. Baston 1824).[3]

---

1   Quoted in Gabriel d'Aubarède, *La révolution des saints* (Paris: Gallimard, 1946), 28. The exact provenance of this quote is unclear; d'Aubarede attributes it to Luther's exhortations to the radical Zwickau prophets after his Invocavit sermons.

2   D'Aubarède, 20.

3   Guillaume-André-Réné Baston, *Jean Bockelson, ou le Roi de Münster: fragment historique* (Paris, 1824), 93, 139.

Too many people are ignorant of the fact that communism has already entered the realm of history as practical fact, that it proved itself, that it prevailed for a few years and was fiercely established in a few provinces, no more than three hundred years ago ... There existed the same pretexts as at present, more or less the same tendencies, the implementation of the same methods for action, but with a mighty means besides, a lever of immense force: the religious and mystical form in which the forceful revolutionaries of the era swathed themselves (*Historical Studies on Communism and Insurrections in the 16th Century*, Arnoul, 1850).[4]

Traces of the tendency toward communism can be found further back in time, before even the development of capitalism. It's the ancient aspiration to recover lost abundance and community.

The first practical attempts at modern communism would themselves be based on remnants of the primitive communism that had survived the development of class societies.

Modern communism draws its inspiration from the works of the ancient advocates for the community of goods: Plato, who endorsed it in the aristocratic style for members of the elite, and the early Christians, who communalized their goods in accordance with the spirit of the Gospels.

However, even while drawing inspiration from and connections to the past, modern communism innovates.

Communism sees itself as an adversary of established society and seeks to replace it. Thomas More devotes the first part of his work to denouncing contemporary ills and to uncovering their causes. He takes note of the ravages visited by the development of capital.

Communism is no longer a state of mind, or a way of life through the

---

4   Albert Arnoul, *Études historiques sur le communisme et les insurrections au XVI siècle* (Melun, 1850), 7-8.

communalization of resources. It's a global and social solution, a method for the organization of production.

Thomas More introduces a navigator, Hythloday, who's visited the imaginary isles of Utopia. Hythloday considers our society:

> My dear More, *spoke he*, to freely own to you what is in my heart, where money is the standard of all things, in those nations, I cannot think either justice or prosperity could prevail in public affairs ... Plato, wise a man as he was, could not but foresee that there was only one way to public salvation, to wit equality, which does not seem to me possible to obtain so long as property belongs to individuals ... I am persuaded, from whence, that there can be no equitable nor just distribution of things, nor can the affairs of men be happily managed, unless property is totally abolished.[5]

More denounces the damages incurred by the development of landed property and plantation capitalism, which drives out peasants to replace them with sheep: "... your sheep, so mild, so easily kept in feed, now may be said to be so rapacious and so wild that they devour men."[6] He denounces the impotence of politics and the distance that necessarily separates good precepts from their practical application.

In Utopia, things are different:

> Every father of a family goes and takes whatsoever he or his family need, without paying for it, without compensation of any sort. Why deny any thing to any person, when there is such plenty, and no man fears that his neighbor might ask more than he needs? For what should make any

---

5   Thomas More, *Utopia*, trans. Gilbert Burnet (Dublin, 1737), 39-40. This and all proceeding *Utopia* quotations have been edited, diverging significantly from Burnet's language to better match the French edition originally cited.

6   More, 14.

act such, if they are all sure that they will be always supplied? What engenders greed or rapaciousness is the fear of want …

In all other places, whereas people talk of a greater good, every man only seeks his own good; but there where no man has any property, all men do pursue the good of the public; and indeed, as the individual good is truly intertwined with the greater good … In Utopia, where every man has a right to every thing, they do all know that no private man can want any thing, if care is taken to keep the public stores full. For among them there is no unequal distribution; there's no poor nor beggar to be seen, and though no man has any thing, yet they are all rich …

Is not a society both unjust and ungrateful, when it is so prodigal of its favors to those that are called gentlemen, or goldsmiths, or such others that are idle or live by flattery, or by contriving the arts of vain pleasure? When, on the other hand, it has neither thought nor feeling toward those of a meaner sort, such as ploughmen, colliers, and smiths, without whom no society could exist? In its selfish cruelty, it exploits the vigor of their youth to extract from them the greatest travail and profit; but after the public has been served by them, and that they come to be oppressed with age, sickness, and want, all their labors and the good that they have done is forgotten, and all the recompense given them is that they are left to die of hunger.[7]

More concludes his book as follows: "there are many things in the commonwealth of Utopia that I wish to see followed in our cities. I wish, not hope."[8] And in everyday language, the word utopia does designate an unfeasible dream. And yet…

---

7   More, 62, 134, 136.
8   More, 140.

And yet, a little over a century later, there would transpire an experiment remarkably close to More's dream. It's rare indeed for a social project to be so faithfully realized.

Guarani communism

The year that *Utopia* was published, the Spaniards invaded and began conquering Paraguay, the land of the Guarani Indians. In the 16th century, the name "Paraguay" designated the Guarani homelands, a territory larger than present-day Paraguay, which is why the experiment we're about to speak of happened beyond the borders of modern Paraguay.

Under the aegis of the Jesuits, hundreds of thousands of Indians would live—cultivate the land, extract and forge metals, set up dockyards, dedicate themselves to the arts—without the establishment of money, wage labor, or private property. The republic of the Guaranis would endure for around a century and a half, then break down with the expulsion of the Jesuits and attacks from the Spaniards and the Portuguese. In its era, this entity constituted the most industrially advanced country in Latin America. Contemporaries would ponder and debate the nature and scope of the experiment that would come to fortify European socialism. Some would see it as a trailblazing attempt; others would play it down or reduce it to a seedy Jesuit enterprise. Over time, this affair would be considered either too Jesuitical or too communist to merit attention.

The documents cited by Clovis Lugon, papist and Stalinophile, make it possible to form a more accurate opinion (*The Republic of the Guaranis*, Éditions Ouvrières, 1970):

Nothing seemed more beautiful to me than the order and the manner in which is administered the needs of the tribe's inhabitants. Those who take in the harvest are obliged to transport all the grain into public stores; there are people appointed to the watch of these stores, who maintain a register of all they receive. At the commencement of each month, the officers who have the management of the grain deliver to the local chiefs the amount necessary for all the families of their districts, and these distribute it forthwith to those families, giving each one more or less grain in accordance with the greater or lesser number therein (Rev'd Fr. Florentin, "Voyage to the West Indies...").[9]

Most of the work was done communally, and the Indians didn't seem tempted by private property. For themselves, they'd keep only chickens or a horse. Individual parcels were distributed so as to encourage them to progress toward private property, but on the day that the Indians had to see to these plots, they stayed "stretched out on their hammocks all day"[10]:

Fr. Cardiel who, as has been said, deplores the persistence of the communist system, did everything possible on his part to lead the Guaranis to private property, and first of all to a sense of profit and individual interest, by encouraging them to cultivate valuable products on their parcels, with a view toward sales of the surplus. He confesses his failure frankly, and professes to having met no more than three examples, all in all, where individuals had taken from their plots a little of sugar or cotton for sale. More, one of these three individuals was a converted mulatto ...

Fr. Cardiel adds: "In the twenty-eight years that I found myself among them, as priest or as compañero, I did not encounter another such

---

9   Florentin de Bourges, "Voyages aux Indes orientales [...]" in *Lettres édifiantes et curieuses* vol. 5 (17): 235-236, quoted in Clovis Lugon, *La république communiste chrétienne des Guaranis, 1610-1768* [The communist Christian republic of the Guaranis] (Paris: Éditions Ouvrières, 1949), 147.

10   Anton Sepp, *Reißbeschreibung, wie dieselbe aus Hispanien in Paraquariam kommen* [...] (Nürnberg, 1697), 302, quoted in Lugon, 140.

example among so many thousands of Indians."[11]

All the Indians were obliged to participate in manual work, and the time they spent on it was limited—a third or a half of the day.

"Everywhere, there are workshops of gilders, of painters, of sculptors, of goldsmiths, of watchmakers, of locksmiths, of carpenters, of joiners, of weavers, of smelters; in a word, of all the arts and all the trades that can be useful to them" (Charlevoix). "One can find so many master artisans and artists only in a great European city" (Garsch). "They make watches, they draw plans, they etch geographical maps" (Sepp).[12]

According to Charlevoix, the Guaranis

succeed, as if by instinct, in all the arts to which they are applied ... They have been seen to make the most elaborate organs upon a single inspection, as well as astronomical spheres, carpets in the Turkish style, and all that is most difficult in the making ... As soon as children are of an age to be able to start working, they are led to these workshops and installed in those for which they seem to have the most inclination, because they are convinced that art must be guided by nature.[13]

The Indians also manufactured bells, their own firearms, cannon and munitions. Printing presses made it possible to release books in several languages, and especially in Guarani. The Indians were militarily organized: "We could immediately mobilize more than thirty thousand Indians, all on

---

11   Lugon, 148, 130.

12   Pierre François Xavier de Charlevoix, *Histoire du Paraguay* (Paris, 1756), 242, quoted in Lugon, 114; Bruno Garsch, *Der Einfluss Der Jesuiten-missionen* [...] [The Influence of the Jesuit Missions] (Breslau: Frankes Verlag und Druckerei, O. Borgmeyer, 1934), 122, quoted in Lugon, 114; Sepp, 22, quoted in Lugon, 114.

13   Charlevoix, 241-42, quoted in Lugon, 115-16.

horseback," and capable "as much of holding a musket as of brandishing a saber ... of fighting in offense or in defense, just like any European" (Sepp). Fr. d'Aguilar, Jesuit general superior of the Republic, wrote: "What could one set against twenty thousand Indians who have measured themselves against the best of Spanish and Portuguese troops, before whom the Mamelukes no longer dare show themselves, who have twice driven out the Portuguese of the Santisimo Sacramento colony, and who for so many years have kept at bay the infidel nations by which they are surrounded?"[14]

According to Charlevoix, there was "neither gold nor silver but for decorating the altars." "The population procured foodstuffs with neither money nor any pieces of coin," says Muratori; "these idols of avarice were absolutely unknown to them."[15]

The value of goods was expressed in "pesos" and "reals" in a purely fictitious way. It was a way of fixing the relative value of everyday foodstuffs ... Apart from barter and the fictional currency of the peso, there existed a 'real' currency consisting of certain goods of general use, which all accepted as payment, even without having immediate need or purpose of it. [Tea, tobacco, honey, corn ...] Prices normally corresponded to the real value of the goods, that being to the sum of labor exacted by their production, without augmentation for the profit of nonexistent intermediaries. The relative price of a particular merchandise was naturally influenced by its rarity or its abundance (Lugon).[16]

---

14 Sepp, 142, quoted in Lugon, 83; Charlevoix, 74, quoted in Lugon, 84.

15 Charlevoix, n.p., quoted in Lugon, 127; Ludovico Antonio Muratori, *Relation des missions du Paraguay* [An Account of the Paraguayan Missions] (Paris, 1826), 152, quoted in Lugon, 127.

16 Lugon, 127-28.

The dealings between the "reductions"[17] were the purview of the community. "As statistics regularly indicated the extent of the reserves and the needs of each reduction, it was easy to predict the exchanges. The vicar held counsel with the corregidor and the majordomo in order to determine the kind and the amount of goods to import and export" (Lugon).[18]

Does this scream *genuine communism?*

Guarani communism wasn't a pure communism. There was the churchy spirit of the Jesuits, the tributes paid to the Spanish crown and the Guarani military forces placed at its service, the persistence of the barter, etc. But we aren't in search of purity.

It wasn't the Jesuits who brought communism to the Guaranis. They found it there already and had to adapt to it. Some were delighted, finding it consistent with the spirit of the Gospels; others, by inclination or under outside pressure, sought to curtail it. The Jesuits permitted the grafting of Western technologies and knowledge onto an ineradicable primitive communism. They permitted the Guarani groups to unite into a consequential whole.

This was a communism sufficient to arouse mistrust and provoke attack. Subject as they were to an authority external to the Guarani community, the Jesuits played a rather detrimental role, in sowing confusion and disunity among the Indians, when the Spanish and the Portuguese attacked the eastern "reductions" from 1754 to 1756. "The Fathers of the reductions had received from the General of the Company, Ignace Visconti, 'the strict order to submit to the inevitable and bring the Indians to obedience'" (Lugon).[19] Menaced directly, Indians fought but were ultimately crushed. The Jesuits were expelled in 1768. Anti-Guarani incursions continued, destroying

---

17   Religious settlements among the Spanish and Roman Catholic colonial missions.

18   Lugon, 129.

19   Lugon, 238.

the experiment. The weakness of Guarani communism was that it wasn't a revolutionary communism to begin with, that it wasn't formed from confrontation.

In 1852, Martin de Moussy wrote:

... this strange regime ... this communism so criticized, perhaps with a semblance of reason; the best proof that it suited the Indians is that the successors of the Jesuits saw themselves forced to continue it nearly to the present day, and that its destruction, not readied by intelligent and fatherly measures, had no other result but that of throwing the Indians into destitution. At this present hour, their last heirs sorely mourn this regime, no doubt imperfect, but so well suited to their instincts and their mores.[20]

Lugon, who absolutely wanted to make the Jesuits out as the importers of communism, further wrote:

In the aftermath of the destruction of Entre Rios, the survivors were reorganized under the leadership of three caciques assisted by a council, completely in accordance with the customs bestowed by the Jesuits. The population of that colony was estimated at 10,000 people between 1820 and 1827. The community of goods was entirely restored. In the reductions falling within modern Paraguay, the communist regime was officially abolished in 1848 by the dictator Lopez. The Guaranis who still remained in the region were at that point stripped of their properties and their goods. They were left to vegetate on reservations established in the North American manner.[21]

---

20 Martin de Moussy, *Mémoire historique sur la décadence et la ruine des missions des Jésuites dans la bassin de la Plata* [An Historical Thesis on the Decline and Ruin of the Jesuit Missions in the Plata Basin] (Paris, 1864), 63-64.

21 Lugon, 263.

The republic of the Guaranis isn't the only example of encounters between Indian communism and the West. There were some others of lesser importance: the Chiquitano republic in southeastern Bolivia, the republic of the Mojeño in northern Bolivia, the group of the Pampas...[22]

The communists of Müntzer and of Paraguay went further than did the Communards, or other modern-day proletarians, by creating an intermediate social form between primitive communism and advanced communism. Would there have been regression with time? It's the power of capital and the resulting degradation, on the level of the social orientation of individuals, that's risen up against communism. There's no regression, only a cycle that's coming to pass—and which will see communism reemerge, this time at the center of the capitalist world.

Maybe this is incomprehensible to those who see history as a linear and continuous process. There's neither regression nor anticipation, but rather a perpetual progress from inferior to superior. But why, then, did modern industry develop from the backwardness of European feudalism, and from neither the great Inca textile mills nor the arts and technologies of China? Why was it only possible to introduce this industry after a period of decline?

In the wake of the bourgeois revolutions, alongside and subsequent to this communism that was swathed in religion—albeit iconoclastic beside the German insurgents, or Campanella, who sought the end of the family— would develop a naturalistic and anti-religious communism.

The Levellers

In England, after the revolution of 1648, a current favorable to communism developed within the party of the "Levellers." Several communist works

---

22 Various regions colonized by the Jesuits.

appeared during this period. These advocated for the universal obligation to work and the free distribution of goods.

Contact with non-Western societies nourished philosophical reflections. In 1704, Guedeville published *Dialogues or Discussions Between a Savage and the Baron de Lahontan*.[23] The Indian was supposed to be superior to the European because he was ignorant of the distinction between *mine* and *thine*.

In 1755, Morelly published his *Code of Nature*. In it, he asserts that man is neither vicious nor wicked. It's necessary to break with property and the "desire to have":

> Now, if you were to take away property, the blind and pitiless self-interest that accompanies it, you would cause all the prejudices in errors that they sustain to collapse. There would be no more resistance, either offensive or defensive, among men; there would be no more furious passions, ferocious actions, notions or ideas of moral evil.[24]

Despite his faith in human nature, Morelly contradictorily proceeds to define laws to govern peoples' lives, down to the smallest detail. Clothing, marriage, divorce, child-rearing, thought, and even daydreams are strictly regulated.

Morelly's communism would especially influence the revolutionary Gracchus Babeuf, who was executed in 1797 after the failure of the Conspiracy of the Equals.

He was fundamentally correct to judge that communism corresponds to

---

23 Louis Armand de Lom d'Arce, baron de Lahontan, *Dialogues de Monsieur le baron de Lahontan et d'un Sauvage* (Amsterdam, 1704). Nicolas Gueudeville immediately published an infamous forgery of this travelogue, so widely read as to have misled critics a century in the future into concluding that Lahontan was a satirical character or pen name of Gueudeville's – as this text does.

24 Étienne-Gabriel Morelly, *Code of Nature*, trans. Ronald Sanders, in Albert Fried and Ronald Sanders, eds., *Socialist Thought: A Documentary History* (New York: Columbia University Press, 1964), 19.

human nature, that it's the natural state of the species. This isn't because man is automatically good or moral, nor because societies succeed one another without modifying some unalterable human nature. Simply put, classes, property, exchange, and the State impose themselves as necessities that are social and therefore also human, but they're only momentary necessities, corresponding to the passage from one communist social form to another. Communism doesn't impose itself. It springs forth unceasingly, even if it can only flourish at certain moments. We've seen that spontaneous and characteristically human manifestations, like speech, have remained communist, at least on the level of form. With understanding itself, communism remains much more simple and transparent than capitalism—the dominant social form. This is because even today, it's a more immediate reality. When we make mockery of bourgeois wealth that's built on hoarding and expressed in money, when we pretend at naivety, it's because we can directly draw on a communist conception of wealth that's extant in a latent state.

People will reproach us for being simplistic or naive. To some extent, these are virtues that we're cultivating. Blessed are the simple of spirit, for theirs is the kingdom of heaven; and not only that. People reproach communism, not for being incomprehensible or unacceptable, but for being naive, for taking no account of the reality it claims to be able to overthrow. But people fight against communism because they know that it's not so naive— that the means for its success exist.

Theory is a necessity. It's necessary in a world where human reality eludes men. But if theory only serves to complicate things, to reinforce the screen that separates men from their humanity, then it's best to abstain. Revolutionary theory isn't like the theory of relativity. It speaks to a reality whose waters we're swimming in. The complexity and the distance that it seeks to reduce, in a move that's consequently communist in itself, aren't linked only to physical reasons but to ones that are human and humanly changeable.

It's tempting to either drug yourself with theory and thereby reject life, or to reject theory and drug yourself with practice. The lack of living—the distance from the mechanisms that organize men's lives—don't lead to a will to learn but to a frantic search for images, for possibilities of identification. What matters isn't to understand and thus arrive at the possibility of transforming reality, but to find those responsible—the guilty, the warmongers, the thieves of labor. It's only because of this search for images and the concrete that the system and its managers have been able to focus popular hostility against one or another social group. This perverted need for practice needs to be opposed with analysis, but above all with life itself. You can't cure an addict with words.

Morelly notes: "It is unfortunately all too true that to form a republic of this sort would be just about impossible at the present time."[25] The utopians never grasped the movement that could lead to communism. In those days, the proletariat didn't yet seem like much of an autonomous force. But utopian descriptions had already manifested the historical need for communism and turned it into an immediate demand, as befits its profound nature.

The future isn't a point external to the reality that we're living in. It is this reality; it is its transcendence. Communism is here and everywhere, today and tomorrow, subjectivity and the objective development of productive forces. You cannot, without losing your way, pit communism as utopia against communism as historical movement. One of the great merits of the utopians is that they entertained no illusions about the historical possibility of their project.

It was later that communist reformers like Cabet and Owen would come along, trying to bring their ideas to life by creating small communities or

---

25 Morelly, 19.

institutions that were "communist" or communist-oriented.[26]

The strength of the utopian is that he doesn't get hung up on elaborating a representation of development, on deducing what's to come from what already is. He makes direct predictions. He tackles radically—that is, on the human level—the problems that capitalism engenders and unveils. Problems that humanity will one day be forced to deal with.

Communism asserts itself as utopia, in its discontinuity with the present. It's conceived as a new global equilibrium.

Against this is opposed a sham determinism that reduces development to a continuous process, where each phase is the extension or the plaster-cast reproduction of the preceding phase. The utopian is reduced to a dreamer or a mystical rationalist. His approach and its point of departure aren't understood as part of the movement in question.

Communism is a manifestation of the extension, historically possible and methodical, of the human species' capacities. It's the natural condition of the species—but this nature is historically produced. History itself only orders and rehashes the same materials without, however, treading water or going in circles.

The intermediate phase of class societies, which tends to negate man by making him into an instrument, was itself only rendered possible and necessary by the specific and genetically inscribed characteristics of the species. It's the human capacity to adapt but also to endure, to use tools but also to be used as a tool, that's turned against humanity. This phase, in engendering capitalism and machinery, has signed its own death warrant.

---

26 French politician and philosopher Étienne Cabet (1788-1856); his utopian socialist Icarian Movement aimed to colonize vast swaths of the American West. Welsh industrialist and early socialist thinker Robert Owen (1771-1858), on whose ideas were founded multiple communes, including his own in New Harmony, Indiana.

Scientific socialism

In the 19th century, the antagonism between the bourgeoisie and the proletariat comes to the forefront. Communism makes fewer claims toward reason or philosophy in general. It seeks to integrate itself into and transform reality in practice. The first tendency to arise is one that seeks to start creating communist islands and to proliferate by example, with the eventual consent of the powers that be. The second tendency is one of revolutionary and insurrectionary communism. In France, this comes to be particularly associated with the name of Blanqui:

> Communism, which is the revolution itself, must be wary of the allures of utopia and never separate itself from politics. Previously it was outside of politics; today it finds itself right at its heart. Politics is nothing more than communism's servant ... The day the gag is removed from the mouth of Labour, it will have to be put into that of Capital.[27]

Blanqui sees communism already at work in the capitalist world—albeit too generously, if you ask us:

> Taxes and government itself derive from communism—in its worst form, to be sure, and yet of an absolute necessity ... In the service of capital, association becomes a scourge, so much so that it will not be endured for long. This glorious principle has the privilege of being able only to do good ("Communism, the Future of Society," 1869).[28]

By linking itself openly to the fight of the proletariat, communism takes a decisive step—but it is also perverted. It progressively ceases to be an

---

27 Louis-Auguste Blanqui, "Communism, the Future of Society," trans. Philippe Le Goff, Peter Hallward, and Mitchell Abidor, *The Blanqui Archive*, Kingston University, https://blanqui.kingston.ac.uk.

28 Blanqui, "Communism, the Future of Society."

immediate demand. It becomes a project, a mission, an historical stage cut off from the present. Emptied of its content for the "Levellers" and the "communalists," it's able to become a guise for capital in the 20th century.

"Scientific socialism" was a way to rationalize the historical alienation of communism. In the 19th century, the working class might have acted autonomously, but communism wasn't possible. By proposing political angles and transitional phases, Bray, Marx, and Blanqui enabled all kinds of misrepresentation.

What's missing from the celebrated *Communist Manifesto*, precisely, is communism. In the *Manifesto*, you can find a vindication of the bourgeoisie, an analysis of class struggle, of transitional measures... But it says little on communism itself, and pretty badly at that.

The *Manifesto* was drawn up for the "League of the Just," later to become the "Communist League." Before the arrival of Marx and Engels, this association of German immigrant artisans and workers had been fairly nebulous in doctrine. Weitling, its founder and theoretician, was of a mystical ilk. Marx and Engels would make incontestable progress but also cause a regression, in relation to the League's prior assertion of communism, which was naive but more constructive and, even, more just.

In June 1847, the League's congress defines its intentions in Article I of its Statutes: "The League aims at the emancipation of humanity by spreading the theory of the community of property and its speediest possible practical introduction."[29]

In November 1846 and February 1847, the steering Committee writes to the sections, "You know that communism is a system according to which the Earth must be the common property of all men, according to which each person must work, 'produce,' according to his abilities, and enjoy, 'consume,'

---

29 "Rules of the Communist League (June 1847)," in *Marx/Engels Collected Works*, vol. 6 (London: Lawrence & Wishart, 2010), 585. No attributed translator.

according to his strengths."[30]

Article I of the new Statutes, drawn up by Marx and Engels, places emphasis on the questions of power and domination and defines communism in the negative: "The aim of the League is the overthrow of the bourgeoisie, the rule of the proletariat, the abolition of the old bourgeois society which rests on the antagonism of classes, and the foundation of a new society without classes and without private property."[31]

In *The Cry for Help of the German Youth* (1841), Weitling defines his Christian communism as follows:

> The problem that He [Christ] set himself was the founding of an empire over the whole earth, the freedom of all nations, the community of goods and of labor for all who profess the empire of God. And this is precisely what the communists of today have adopted anew…
>
> There are communists who are such without knowing it: the hard-working farmer who shares his morsel of brown bread with the starving worker is a communist; the hard-working artisan who doesn't swindle his workers, who pays them in proportion to the product of their shared labor, is a communist; the rich man who employs his surplus for the good of long-suffering humanity is a communist…[32]

Communism and charity are practically conflated. Marx would react, vigorously and rightfully, against this slop. But the *Communist Manifesto* no more defines communists by their communism. They're just the most resolute

---

30 Indeterminate source.

31 "Rules of the Communist League (December 1847)," 6:663.

32 *Der Hülferuf der deutschen Jugend*, no. 3, November 1841, in Wilhelm Weitling, *Der Hülferuf der deutschen Jugend, Die junge Generation, 1841-1843* [The Cry for Help of the German Youth, The Young Generation, 1841–1843] (Leipzig: Zentralantiquariat der DDR, 1972) 36, 39.

among proletarians, those who have the advantage of a clear understanding of the proletarian movement's workings: the possessors of theory.

At the end of the 19th century and the beginning of the 20th—and despite Marx's ragings against social democracy, most notably before the Gotha Congress of 1875—communism would be emptied of its true content. It would retain its underlying meaning only for a handful of anarchists.

In 1891, in order to justify "individual reclamation," which is to say theft, Paul Reclus offers this short and sweet definition of communism in *La Révolte*:

> Activity, in the world that we imagine, shall be equally distant from our present ideas of both work and theft: one will take without asking, and this shall not be theft; one will use one's own abilities and faculties, and this will not be work.[33]

With the revolutionary wave that follows the First World War, and in the wake of the Russian Revolution, Marxist and communist tendencies reappear. There are remnants of communism, among the Bolsheviks. Remnants that will quickly be perverted, disappearing with the retreat of the global revolution and their own entanglement in Russia's problems.

It's with good reason that the very premature counterrevolutionary role of the Bolsheviks has been denounced; it's with good reason that the bourgeois character of Lenin's theoretical and practical oeuvre has been brought to light. But it's idiotic to try and hold the Bolsheviks responsible for the failure of the worker's revolution in Russia. Rather, the Bolsheviks are a specific case where a handful of men managed to influence the course of history, to the extreme of the revolutionary possibilities. Their adversaries, even to their left, generally only had humanist and democratic perspectives to oppose.

---

33   Reclus, "Le Travail et le Vol" [Work and Theft], *La Révolte*, no. 9, November 21, 1891.

The contrast between the magnitude of the revolutionary wave and the feebleness of its affirmation of communism is striking.

In Germany and Holland especially, "left-communists" denounce the Russian regime as a capitalism of the State. They counter this with a communism based on workers' management. They're to thank for the emphasis placed on workers' councils and the autonomous action of the masses. This current, notably expressed by the KAPD,[34] will be fragmented with the ebb of the revolution into insignificant sects, where once it was capable of rallying hundreds of thousands of workers.

This worker-managementism will also be put to use by anarchists and anarcho-syndicalists. Communism is reduced to the self-organization of producers.

It's in Italy that the left of Bordiga, which dominates the PCI[35] at its founding, will best restore communist doctrine. It stands against participation in elections, rejects common fronts with social democracy, criticizes the democratic illusion. It foregrounds the abolition of wage labor and the mercantile economy. Particularly after the Second World War, Bordiga elaborates his analysis of the capitalist counterrevolution in Russia as well as his own notion of communism. You don't build communism—you destroy mercantilism.

Despite its great depth, Bordigism never manages to free itself of its Leninist miasma. Its radicalism and insight go to waste in the worst impasses.

After the Second World War, it's only very gradually that theoretical communism is reborn. The prosperity and good health of capital don't help.

---

34 Kommunistische Arbeiterpartei Deutschlands [Communist Workers' Party of Germany], 1920-1933, the left-communist party of the Weimar Republic.

35 Partito Comunista Italiano [Italian Communist Party], 1921-1991; under the leadership of Amadeo Bordiga, among others, it split from the reformist Italian Socialist Party in the wake of the Third International.

After considering and reconsidering its past, and rather poorly anyway, it attempts to move on. It develops gradually, as the social then economic crises of capital start to become visible once more.

After having taken up the critique of the Eastern Bloc and bureaucracy, the Situationists elaborate a theory of modern society based on the commodity and the "spectacle." They denounce modern poverty. But however pertinent their analysis may often be, it stays on the surface of things. Captive in style and content to the spectacular effect that it both denounces and reflects.

The Situationists produce a brilliant and corrosive social critique, but not a theory of capital, nor of the machinery that sustains the spectacle, nor of the revolution. They don't broach the question of communization, other than by applauding the immediate negation of the commodity (looting or burning) or by sinking into councilism (for the absolute power of the workers' councils upon which everything depends). Feral enemies of Bolshevism, they, like the Bolsheviks, turn the revolution into a question of organization.

Communist doctrine needs to be centered on the description of the future and, above all, the process of communization. It's on this that we have to debate, unite, or, on the contrary, divide. It's not a question of fleeing the present but of living it, and judging it by the light of the future. Communism is here, and its prospects can be immediately set against the capitalist mire.

If protest fails to open onto constructive prospects and therefore demonstrates its lack of depth, it becomes a means for wallowing in misery under the pretext of denouncing it. Following the lead of clowns and fools, ideologues end up feeding off the very decomposition of the system. While we might forgive anything of those who make us laugh, we can forgive these people of nothing. It's the ultimate way to mask the gigantic and unexplored possibilities that are opening up before humanity—the ultimate way to extinguish hope in the hearts of the oppressed!

In the course of history, the communist idea and the communist struggle resurface unendingly. They gradually transform, however, as their co-optation by capital forces them to go ever further. Today, as capitalism has normalized public property and penal labor, communism is beyond the opposition of individual and collective appropriation. It's no longer all about the question of property. Communism no longer has to oscillate between an asocial naturalism and an exasperated moralism or regulationism.

The Marxist stage can't be spared, either. Communism was thought of as a mode of production to succeed capitalism. But it's something that's at once more than and different from a social form. It's the movement, present within the very capitalism that represses it, through which human activity smashes its shackles and flourishes at last!

Communist activity

Communism is, first of all, activity. First of all because it arises from within capitalism before it's able to overthrow it. First of all because in the communist world, human activity and the upkeep of vital functions are no longer prisoner to the engendered social forms. The organization of tasks no longer has to be ossified into institutions.

Communism positively springs forth from within capitalism. But it asserts itself as the reverse of negation. Communism as action is at once negation and anticipation. There aren't two successive moments. The more that activity rises up against capital the more it tends to represent communism, and vice versa.

It's therefore not a question of building islands of communism within capitalism. From the communist point of view, when activity tends toward building, it's destroying itself.

There aren't any communist needs that would have to be satisfied outside of the system. Even if there's an element of communism underlying the needs, once they appear they can't be separated from their potential for real-ization, even if imaginary, from inside the system. Capitalism's inability to satisfy desires leads to the world overcoming it and overcoming the desires that it enables.

We don't see anything communist about either moral sensibility, as Weitling does, or the glorious principle of association, as Blanqui does. If that's communism, it's negative communism (though not to be con-fused with bad communism). It's the rise of the movement of capitalist dispossession.

Dispossessed of the instruments of production, denied power over their labor, separated from one another, yet confronted, animating an enormous productive force, united in a great mass—proletarians see communism as negatively inscribed in their circumstances. Even if they do own their own toolboxes, they have no particular interests to champion. Their privation faces up to the might and the social wealth that they fuel. This is what makes the proletariat the class of communism. Proletarians can't reappropriate the means of production piece by piece; they have to communalize them.

But what's fundamental, even if things are inextricably linked, isn't so much the movement of reappropriating and communalizing goods as it is the new activity that develops: the reappropriation of life, the birth of new relationships, the reversal of the relation of domination between men and objects.

Of course communism, the human community, is one stage of historical development, one given mode of production. The antagonisms that set human groups and interests against each other will disappear.

But you can't understand communism if you turn it into a finalized goal or movement, detached from the activity that produces it. In subjugating the activity to the goal, the means to the ends, you're only projecting onto history the way that commodity-capital dominates human activity, which it imprisons in the labor-form. The communist goal, result, and social form needs to be considered as a necessity of activity, seeking to safeguard and reproduce its conditions of existence.

Community exists in the society to come—the unification of the planet, the end of the division of the economy into enterprises—in a solution that's global and social. But those who don't see it at work in the spontaneous action of the proletarians, in the immediate and specific negations of racism and lies, can't understand anything about it.

The relation between immediate action and the world to come is central. The universality of communism is contained within the specifics of real circumstances.

If universality can spring up from the specific, it's because this specificity is itself the product of the universal, unifying, and privative logic of capital.

Those who don't grasp the connection are obliged to resort to a false universal: the (proletarian!) party, the (proletarian!) State, or even the pro-letariat itself, but only in its capacity as an abstraction or representation. This false universal is itself considered to harbor the active ingredient, before an inert social ointment. The instrument and its object. The spirit transforming or straddling matter.

Communist consciousness only becomes widespread when society is shaken to its foundations. But all is already present in the life that springs up, including consciousness, which ceases to be the passive reflection of frozen representations and circumstances. Ideological consciousness is transformed into practical consciousness. In this, it's already communist.

The more the struggle intensifies, the more those who take part in it find themselves cleansed of the prejudices and pettinesses that used to occupy them. Their consciousness comes unsnarled, and the gaze that they cast on reality and the existence that they lead is one that's new and astonished.

This presence of communism doesn't imply a monopoly on struggle, in the narrow sense of the term—a clear and overt clash between labor and capital. It manifests itself through all social life and often deserts those ritualized, rigid, boring struggles that are no longer struggles at all.

True human community always entails a contradiction to capital. It moves toward becoming open struggle or it sees itself destroyed, co-opted in order to be made into an image for papering over reality. Capital's tightening hold on life is increasingly repressive, rendering impossible all humanity, all love, all true creation and inquiry. Men are becoming empty carcasses, trudging lifelessly to the rhythm of capital. Revolt and reaction therefore need to take on an increasingly human character. This humanity— contradictory to capital, the precise phase in the becoming of our species—is what we call communist. This label will remain necessary so long as this human becoming can't yet claim to represent and encompass all human embodiment because it remains antagonistic to capital.

Communism is possible because capital can't transform men into robots. Even if it automates their existence, it can't do without their humanity. The most assimilationist and servile of activities feed off participation, creation, and initiative, even if these qualities can't truly flourish. The need for and expectation of a wage aren't enough to keep the worker going. He needs other motivations; he has to make his own contributions. The labor form can't vacate the generic, human character of the worker's activity.

We've seen (Ch. 4) that beneath these divisions, life goes on and maintains its wholeness; it's impossible to completely dissociate production, education, and experimentation. In production, even the most stupid job requires a certain adaptivity from its worker, the ability to cope with unplanned circumstances. Likewise, the most abstract education must be made tangible through certain "products," even if they're only exam papers. The necessities of outside testing fall back on production...

The system of production would cave in if workers were no longer able to experiment, to help each other out, to consult each other. The hierarchical organization of labor can only survive if its own rules are flouted all the time. It imposes an insurmountable framework on these illegalities, and on the spontaneous activity of workers, in order to prevent them from developing and becoming truly dangerous and subversive. When a breach opens up or a conflict breaks out, this activity moves to become autonomous and develop its own logic.

By struggling, the proletarian immediately negates himself as wage laborer, as slave, as robot. However limited this reappearance of life and activity may be, capitalist oppression is already being found guilty at its very foundations.

The proletarian, who had been no more than a cog, begins once more to choose, to take part, to take risks. He retakes control of his conduct. His eyes open; his intellect thaws. The oppressive seriousness, the monotony that smothers men in the work camps of wage labor, the policed and commodified world—they cave in. Everything becomes possible once more.

Revolt, as search for pleasure and efficacy, can already be found beyond work. It wages can be found directly within the joy that it awakens and the results that it wins.

The wildcat activity of the proletariat sees itself suppressed as soon as it surpasses a certain threshold. More frequently, it's co-opted and assimilated until it's dead in the water. So not only is communism the product of capitalism, capitalism is the product of communism. If we make much of this latent communism, still in its first faltering steps, we don't do so in order to fetishize it. It can only be itself by surpassing itself, by tearing itself away from the capitalist orbit. To recognize its significance is in no way to kneel down before a spontaneity that would refuse to organize itself, to be disciplined and go on the offensive.

Capital co-opts in accordance with its innermost nature. It's a vampire by definition. It's therefore not worth marveling over one or another of its more spectacular aspects.

Workers' struggles, despite the opposition that they've aroused, have helped the system to transform itself and to realize its potentialities while always staying true to itself. Struggles for labor and politics, or struggles toward the ends of labor and politics, have shaken up the system and empowered it to modernize.

The struggle is coming to be sterilized at its roots. Strikes, demonstrations, and factory occupations tend toward hot air. People no longer try to harm capital but to inform it of discomfort, to express discontent. At the pinnacle of alienation, the strike no longer even seems like a means of exerting pressure but like a sacrifice on the part of those who walk out. They demonstrate, by the magnitude of their sacrifice, the seriousness of their protest. The social war is replaced by the parade.

The activity and the program

The prospect of action is the prospect of communism. It's not about denying the need for action to be embodied, to be instantiated, to be drawn from what it generates and transforms; on the contrary, capital only considers action from the perspective of the thing produced. This is why, against all evidence, it equates labor with all specifically human action. Activity can be taken seriously only in view of its immediate and positive input. Positive according to capital.

This desire to consider only immediate impacts hides the anticipatory character of the workers' struggle:

> Instead of looking at what workers are doing, bourgeois ideologues try to imagine what workers would like to obtain. Proletarian activity is seen as, at most, an agent of disruption or the modernization of the system, never as the outline of its overthrow.[36]

This activity isn't taken seriously because it doesn't produce anything. It'd be purely destructive and negative. *How is anyone dreaming that it could animate*

---

36 Pomerol and Medoc, *Lordstown 72, ou les déboires de la General Motors* [Lordstown '72, or the woes of General Motors] (Paris: Editions de l'Oubli and Les Amis de 4 Millions de Jeunes Travailleurs, 1977), 21.

a new world? But in reality, the negative character of communist activity is determined by its immediate opportunities and the capitalist context. It's only negative from the perspective of capital, not from the perspective of those who set it in motion.

> We must not delude ourselves on the destructive nature of communist activity, such as it emerges from the flanks of capitalism. It's already producing utility. Sabotage destroys market value by attacking the use that can be made of a commodity, but it produces a use value for the worker, in that it allows them to win free time, to put pressure on the boss (Lordstown '72).[37]

This destructive character vanishes, even, when the worker begins producing for his own benefit on the company dime.

By making revolutionary proletarian activity the crux of our doctrine, we can grasp the similarity and the discontinuity between the revolt against capital and the world to come. We see the contradictory unity of work and communist activity. We can confirm that communism is first a radical transformation of human activity before it's an alteration of social forms. This allows us to reconsider the communist world's traditional conceptions of the evaluation of costs.

In writings from his youth, Marx came to conceive of communism not only as movement but also as activity. Unfortunately, as he elaborated his conception of historical development, this perspective would dim in its capacity as an integrated perspective. Marx would become the communist theoretician of capitalism—in both senses of the expression. Heads, he analyzes capitalism from the perspective of its negation. Tails, he's a prisoner of capitalism.

Obviously, Marx considered human activity as both revolutionary

---

37 Pomerol and Medoc, 27.

activity and productive activity—but separately. Regarding the Revolutions of 1848, he showed that proletarian activity feeds off of its class situation and develops its own logic. In his economic works, he made labor the basis and the measure of value. But by deducting productive activity from the product, he fell back on the false equivalence of labor and human productive activity. He didn't see, in the activity of the revolutionary proletariat, a prospect beyond labor.

If everything lies in the immediate activity of the proletariat, why continue bothering with theory, with organizing? Why try to rework a program?

Not everything lies in the immediate activity of the proletariat, even if everything has to tie back to it, has to be put into perspective and made harmonious. Immediate activity is only communist through its capacity to outstrip itself.

The communist program is a necessity, even if it currently lies severed from the whole of the proletariat. It isn't external to its movement; it's an anticipation, a guide. Its truth lies in its capacity to be dissolved—that is to say, to be realized by that class. It's nothing but the program of proletarian activity.